BRITISH RAILWA

LOCO

C000203294

FORTY-FIRST EDITION
1999

The Complete Guide to all Diesel & Electric
Locomotives which operate on the
Railtrack and Eurotunnel networks

Neil Webster

ISBN 1 902336 03 8

CONTENTS

READERS' COMMENTS

With such a wealth of information as contained in this book, it is inevitable a few inaccuracies may be found. The author will be pleased to receive notification from readers of any such inaccuracies, and also notification of any additional information to supplement our records and thus enhance future editions.

Please send comments to:

Neil Webster,
Platform 5 Publishing Ltd.,
Wyvern House,
Sark Road,
Sheffield,
South Yorkshire,
S2 4HG
Tel: 0114 255 2625
Fax: 0114 255 2471
e-mail: metent@globalnet.co.uk

Both the authors and the staff of Platform 5 regret they are unable to answer specific queries regarding locomotives and rolling stock other than through the 'Q & A' section in the Platform 5 magazine *Today's Railways*.

UPDATES

A comprehensive update to all the books in the *British Railways Pocket Book* series is published every month in the Platform 5 magazine, *Today's Railways*, which also contains news and rolling stock information on the railways of both Britain and Continental Europe. This is the ONLY commercial magazine to contain official Platform 5 rolling stock updates. For further details of *Today's Railways*, please see the advertisements inside the front and back covers of this book.

Information in this edition is intended to illustrate the actual situation on Britain's railways, rather than necessarily agree with TOPS, RSL and other computer records. Information is updated to 30 November 1998.

ORGANISATION & OPERATION OF BRITAIN'S RAILWAY SYSTEM

INFRASTRUCTURE & OPERATION

Britain's national railway infrastructure i.e. the track, signalling, stations and associated power supply equipment is owned by a public company – Railtrack PLC. Many stations and maintenance depots are leased to and operated by train operating companies (TOCs), but some larger stations remain under Railtrack control. The only exception is the infrastructure on the Isle of Wight, which is owned by the government and is leased to the Island Line franchisee.

Trains are operated by TOCs over the Railtrack network, regulated by access agreements between the parties involved. In general, TOCs are responsible for the provision and maintenance of the locomotives, rolling stock and staff necessary for the direct operation of services, whilst Railtrack is responsible for the provision and maintenance of the infrastructure and also for staff needed to regulate the operation of services.

DOMESTIC PASSENGER TRAIN OPERATORS

The large majority of passenger trains are operated by the TOCs on fixed term franchises. These are currently as follows:

Franchise	Owner	Trading Name
Anglia Railways	GB Railways	Anglia Railways
InterCity East Coast	Sea Containers	Great North Eastern Railway
InterCity West Coast	Virgin Rail	Virgin Train
Cross Country Trains	Virgin Rail	Virgin Trains
Great Eastern Railway	First Group	First Great Eastern
Great Western Trains	First Group	First Great Western
North West Regional Railways	First Group	First North Western
Midland Main Line	National Express	Midland Mainline

Gatwick Express	National Express	Gatwick Express
North London Railways	National Express	Silverlink Train Services
Central Trains	National Express	Central Trains
ScotRail	National Express	ScotRail
Merseyrail Electrics	MTL Rail	Merseyrail Electrics
Regional Railways North East	MTL Rail	Northern Spirit
LTS Rail	Prism Rail	LTS Rail
South Wales & West	Prism Rail	Wales & West Passenger Trains
Cardiff Railway	Prism Rail	Cardiff Railways
West Anglia Great Northern	Prism Rail	WAGN
South West Trains	Stagecoach	South West Trains
Island Line	Stagecoach	Island Line
Network South Central	Connex Rail	Connex South Central
South Eastern Trains	Connex Rail	Connex South Eastern
Thameslink Rail	GOVIA	Thameslink Rail
Chiltern Railways	M40 Trains	Chiltern Railways
Thames Trains	Victory Rail	Thames Trains

The above companies may also operate other services under 'Open Acces arrangements.

The following operators run non-franchised services only:

Operator	Trading Name	Route
British Airports Authority	Heathrow Express	London Paddington–Heathrow Airpor
West Coast Railway	West Coast Railway	Fort William–Mallaig

INTERNATIONAL PASSENGER OPERATIONS

Eurostar (UK) operates international passenger services between the Unite Kingdom and continental Europe, jointly with French National Railways (SNCI and Belgian National Railways (SNCB/NMBS). In addition, a service for th conveyance of accompanied road vehicles through the Channel Tunnel is pro vided by the tunnel operating company, Eurotunnel. Eurostar (UK) is a sul sidiary of London & Continental Railways, which is now jointly owned by N₁ tional Express Group and the British Airports Authority.

FREIGHT TRAIN OPERATIONS

TOCs currently engaged in freight train operation are:

English Welsh & Scottish Railway (EWS)
Freightliner
Direct Rail Services
Mendip Rail

SING THIS BOOK

AYOUT OF INFORMATION

comotives are listed in numerical order of class number, and then in nu-
erical order of individual locomotives – using current numbers as allocated
the Rolling Stock Library. Where numbers carried are different to those
ficially allocated (e.g. former numbers); these are noted in class headings
here appropriate.

ch locomotive entry is laid out as in one of the following examples:

unting Locomotives

L No.	Detail	Livery	Owner	Pool	Depot	Location
3179		**WA**	WA	HQXX	HE	Hornsey EMUD

ain Line Locomotives

L No.	Detail	Livery	Owner	Pool	Depot	Name
777	x	**RX**	E	WHDP	CD	Restored

LASS HEADINGS

incipal details and dimensions are quoted for each class in metric and/or
nperial units as considered appropriate bearing in mind common usage in
e UK. The following abbreviations are used:

c.	alternating current
R	British Railways
ARMD	Carriage Maintenance Depot
S	Carriage Sidings
SD	Carriage Servicing Depot
c.	direct current
LT	Freightliner Terminal
p	horsepower
z	Hertz
N	kilonewtons
m/h	kilometres per hour
W	kilowatts
of	pounds force
.	metres
m.	millimetres
ph	miles per hour
CH	Railway Clearing House
om	revolutions per minute
D	Servicing Depot
	tonnes
&RSMD	Traction & Rolling Stock Maintenance depot
MD	Traction Maintenance Depot
	volts
VRD	Wagon Repair Depot

All dimensions and weights are quoted for locomotives in an 'as new' condition with all necessary supplies (e.g. oil, water and sand) on board. Dimensions are quoted in the order Length – Width – Height. All lengths quoted are over buffers or couplings as appropriate. All width and height dimensions quoted are maxima.

DETAIL DIFFERENCES

Only detail differences which currently affect the areas and types of train which locomotives may work are shown. All other detail differences are specifically excluded – details of these may be found in more specialist publications. Where such differences occur within a class or part class, these are shown alongside the individual locomotive number. Standard abbreviations used are:

a	Train air brake equipment only
c	Scharfenberg couplers
j	RCH jumper cables for operating with Propelling Control Vehicles
m	Multiple working equipment
p	Train air, vacuum and electro-pneumatic brakes
r	Radio Electronic Token Block (RETB) equipment
s	Slow Speed Control equipment
v	Train vacuum brake only
x	Train air and vacuum brakes ('Dual brakes')
+	Additional fuel tank capacity
§	Sandite laying equipment.

In all cases use of the above abbreviations indicates the equipment indicated is normally operable. Meaning of non-standard abbreviations and symbols is detailed in individual class headings.

LIVERY CODES

Livery codes are used in this publication to denote the various liveries carried by locomotives. Readers should note it is impossible in a publication of this size to list every livery variation which currently exists. In particular items ignored for the purposes of this book include:

*   Minor colour variations;
*   All numbering, lettering and branding;
*   Omission of logos.

The descriptions quoted are thus a general guide only and may be subject to slight variation between individual locomotives. Logos as appropriate for each livery are normally deemed to be carried. A full list of livery codes used in this publication appears on page 89.

OWNER CODES

Owner codes are used in this publication to denote the owners of locomotives listed. Many locomotives are leased by the TOCs from specialist leasing companies. A full list of owner codes used in this publication appears on page 91.

POOL CODES

Locomotives are split into operational groups ('pools') for diagramming and maintenance purposes. The official codes used to denote these pools are shown in this publication.

A full list of pool codes used in this publication appears on page 92.

DEPOT & LOCATION CODES

Depot codes are used in this publication to denote the normal maintenance base of each operational locomotive. However, maintenance may be carried out at other locations and may also be carried out by mobile maintenance teams.

Location codes are used in this publication to denote the current actual location of stored vehicles. A location code will be followed by (S) to denote stored.

A full list of depot and location codes used in this publication appears on page 95.

SHUNTING LOCOMOTIVE LOCATIONS

The actual location of operational shunting locomotives, updated to the date of going to press, is included as a guide to readers as to where these locomotives may be found. Whilst some locomotives remain at certain locations for some considerable length of time, others may move around far more frequently. Readers must appreciate the listing of a locomotive at a location is no absolute guarantee the locomotive concerned (or any other locomotive) will remain present on a subsequent date.

NAMES

Only names carried with official sanction are listed in this publication. As far as possible names are shown in UPPER/lower case characters as actually shown on the name carried on the locomotive.

GENERAL INFORMATION

CLASSIFICATION AND NUMBERING

All locomotives are classified and allocated numbers under the TOPS numbering system, introduced in 1972. This comprises a two-digit class number followed by a three-digit serial number. Where the actual number carried by a locomotive differs from the allocated number, or where an additional number is carried to the allocated number, this is shown by a note in the class heading.

For diesel locomotives, class numbers offer an indication of engine hors
power as shown in the table below. However, it should be noted this syste
is no longer an infallible indicator of engine horsepower (e.g. Class 57).

Engine hp	Class No. Range
0–799	01–14
800–1000	15–20
1001–1499	21–31
1500–1999	32–39
2000–2999	40–54
3000+	55 onwards.

For electric locomotives class numbers are allocated in ascending numeric
order under the following scheme:

Class 70–80   direct current and dc/diesel dual system locomotives.
Class 81 onwards   alternating current and ac/dc dual system locomotives.

Preserved locomotives authorised to run on the Railtrack system are allo
cated numbers in the Classes 89 and 98. Details of these numbers are n
shown in this book as such numbers relate to computer transactions only ar
are not generally carried externally by the locomotives concerned. Full d
tails of all preserved locomotives can be found in the Platform 5 book *Pr
served Locomotives of British Railways*.

WHEEL ARRANGEMENT

For main line diesel and electric locomotives the system whereby the numb
of driven axles on a bogie or frame is denoted by a letter (A = 1, B = 2, C =
etc.) and the number of undriven axles is denoted by a number is used. Th
use of a letter 'o' after a letter indicates each axle is individually powere
whilst the + symbol indicates bogies are intercoupled.

For shunting locomotives, the Whyte notation is used. In this notation, gene
ally used in Britain for steam locomotives, the number of leading wheels a
given, followed by the number of driving wheels and then the trailing wheel

HAULAGE CAPABILITY OF DIESEL LOCOMOTIVES

The haulage capability of a diesel locomotive depends basically upon thre
factors:

1. Its adhesive weight. The greater the weight on its driving wheels, the great
the adhesion and thus more tractive power can be applied before wheelsli
occurs.

2. The characteristics of its transmission. To start a train the locomotive has t
exert a pull at standstill. A direct drive diesel engine cannot do this, hence th
need for transmission. This may be mechanical, hydraulic or electric. Th
current British Standard for locomotives is electric transmission. Here the dies
engine drives a generator or alternator and the current produced is fed to th
traction motors. The force produced by each driven wheel depends on th
current in its traction motor. In other words, the larger the current, the harde
it pulls.

As the locomotive speed increases, the current in the traction motor falls, hence the *Maximum Tractive Effort* is the maximum force at its wheels the locomotive can exert at a standstill. The electrical equipment cannot take such high currents for long without overheating. Hence the *Continuous Tractive Effort* is quoted which represents the current which the equipment can take continuously.

3. The power of its engine. Not all power reaches the rail, as electrical machines are approximately 90% efficient. As the electrical energy passes through two such machines (the generator or alternator and the traction motors), the *Power at Rail* is approximately 81% (90% of 90%) of the engine power, less a further amount used for auxiliary equipment such as radiator fans, traction motor blowers, air compressors, battery charging, cab heating, Electric Train Supply (ETS) etc. The power of the locomotive is proportional to the tractive effort times the speed. Hence when on full power there is a speed corresponding to the continuous tractive effort.

HAULAGE CAPABILITY OF ELECTRIC LOCOMOTIVES

Unlike a diesel locomotive, an electric locomotive does not develop it power on board and its performance is determined only by two factors, namely its weight and the characteristics of its electrical equipment. Whereas a diesel locomotive tends to be a constant power machine, the power of an electric locomotive varies considerably. Up to a certain speed it can produce virtually a constant tractive effort. Hence power rises with speed according to the formula given in section three above, until a maximum speed is reached at which tractive effort falls, such that the power also falls. Hence the power at the speed corresponding to the maximum tractive effort is lower than the maximum speed.

BRAKE FORCE

The brake force is a measure of the braking power of a locomotive. This is shown on the locomotive data panels so operating staff can ensure sufficient brake power is available on freight trains.

ELECTRIC TRAIN SUPPLY (ETS)

A number of locomotives are equipped to provide a supply of electricity to the train being hauled to power auxiliaries such as heating, cooling fans, air conditioning and kitchen equipment. ETS is provided from the locomotive by means of a separate alternator, except in the case of Class 33 which have a dc generator. The ETS index of a locomotive is a measure of the electrical power available for train supply.

Similarly all loco hauled coaches also have an ETS index, which in this case is a measure of the power required to operate equipment mounted in the coach. The sum of the ETS indices of all the hauled vehicles in a train must not exceed the ETS index of the locomotive.

ETS is commonly known as ETH (Electric Train Heating), which is a throwbac
to the days before loco-hauled coaches were equipped with electrically pow
ered auxiliary equipment.

ROUTE AVAILABILITY (RA)

This is a measure of a railway vehicle's axle load. The higher the axle load c
a vehicle, the higher the RA number on a scale from 1 to 10. Each Railtrac
route has a RA number and in general no vehicle with a higher RA numbe
may travel on that route without special clearance.

MULTIPLE & PUSH-PULL WORKING

Multiple working between locomotives (i.e. between two and five locomo
tives being driven from one cab) is provided by jumper cables connecting th
locomotives. However, not all types are compatible with each other, and
number of different systems are in use, each system being incompatible wit
any other.

Blue Star Coupling Code: Classes 20/0, 20/9, 31, 33, and 37. Locomotive
47971 and 47976.
DRS System: Classes 20/3 and 37/6.
GM System: Classes 59, 66, and 67.
Green Circle Coupling Code: Class 47 (not all equipped).
Orange Square Coupling Code: Class 50.
Red Diamond Coupling Code: Classes 56 and 58.
SR System: Classes 33/1, 73 and various 750 V d.c. EMUs.
Within Own Class only: Classes 43 and 60.

Class 47s nos. 47701–47717 use a time-division multiplex (TDM) system fo
push-pull working which utilises the existing Railway Clearing House (RCH
jumper cables between coaches. Previously these cables had only been used
to control train lighting and public address systems.

A number of other locomotives are equipped with a more modern TDM sys
tem for push-pull working which also facilitates multiple working.

1. LOCOMOTIVES

1.1 DIESEL LOCOMOTIVES

CLASS 03   BR/GARDNER   0-6-0

Built: 1962 by BR at Swindon Works.
Engine: Gardner 8L3 of 152 kW (204 hp) at 1200 rpm.
Transmission: Mechanical. Fluidrive type 23 hydraulic coupling to Wilson-Drewry CA5R7 gearbox with SCG type RF11 final drive.
Max. Tractive Effort: 68 kN (15300 lbf).
Cont. Tractive Effort: 68 kN (15300 lbf) at 3.75 mph.
Train Brakes: Air & vacuum.
Brake Force: 13 t.
Weight: 31.3 t.
Design Speed: 28.5 mph.
Fuel Capacity: 1364 litres.
Train Supply: Not equipped.

Dimensions: 7.93 x 2.59 x 3.73 m.
Wheel Diameter: 1092 mm.
Max. Speed: 28.5 mph.
RA: 1.
Multiple Working: Not equipped.

| 3179 | **WN** WN HQXX | HE | *Hornsey T&RSMD* |

Name: 03179   CLIVE

CLASS 08   BR/ENGLISH ELECTRIC   0-6-0

Built: 1955–62 by BR at Crewe, Darlington, Derby, Doncaster or Horwich Works.
Engine: English Electric 6KT of 298 kW (400 hp) at 680 rpm.
Main Generator: English Electric 801.
Traction Motors: Two English Electric 506.
Max. Tractive Effort: 156 kN (35000 lbf).
Cont. Tractive Effort: 49 kN (11100 lbf) at 8.8 mph.
Power At Rail: 194 kW (260 hp).
Brake Force: 19 t.
Weight: 49.6–50.4 t.
Design Speed: 20 mph.
Fuel Capacity: 3037 litres.
Train Supply: Not equipped.

Train Brakes: Air & vacuum.
Dimensions: 8.92 x 2.59 x 3.89 m.
Wheel Diameter: 1372 mm.
Max. Speed: 15 mph.
RA: 5.
Multiple Working: Not equipped.

Non-standard liveries/numbering:
- 08375/519/730/867 are BR style black.
- 08397 is as **F**, but with BR Railfreight General yellow & red logos.
- 08414 is as **DG**, but with BR & Railfreight Distribution logos and large bodyside numbers. Also carries number D3529.
- 08454/887/934 are in Virgin Trains 'Pitstop' livery of black with a large chequered flag on the bodyside.
- 08460 is light grey with black underframes, cab doors, window surrounds and roof. Also carries number D3575.
- 08500 is plain red, lined out in black and white.

- 08527 is light grey with a black roof, blue bodyside stripe and 'Ilford Level 5' branding,
- 08593 is Great Eastern Railway style blue. Also carries number D3760.
- 08601 is London Midland & Scottish Railway style black.
- 08616 is Great Western Railway style green with cast numberplate 3783.
- 08617 is in Virgin Trains 'Pitstop' livery of black with a large red and white bodyside flag.
- 08642 is London & South Western Railway style black. Also carries number D3809.
- 08649 is grey with blue, white and red stripes and WTL logo. Also carries number D3816.
- 08682 is dark blue with a grey roof.
- 08689 is as **DG**, but with BR Railfreight General yellow & red logos and large bodyside numbers.
- 08715 is 'Dayglo' orange.
- 08721 is as **B**, but with a red and yellow stripe.
- 08724 is RFS style blue livery.
- 08743/903 are ICI Trafalgar blue.
- 08785 is silver grey.
- 08793 is LNER style apple green.
- 08805 is London Midland & Scottish Railway style maroon. Also carries number 3973.
- 08830 carries number D3998.
- 08870 is RMS Locotech blue and red. Also carries RMS number 024.
- 08879 is green and black with Railfreight Distribution logos.
- 08883 is Caledonian Railway style blue.
- 08907 is London & North Western Railway style black.
- 08928 is as **FR**, with large bodyside numbers and light blue solebar.
- 08938 is grey and red.

Notes: † – Equipped with remote control.

Class 08/0. Standard Design.

08077	**RF**	RF	DFLS	EH	Southampton Maritime FLT
08331	**GN**	RF	MBDL	ZB	Hays Chemicals, Sandbach
08375	**0**	MO	MBDL	SD	Sellafield TMD
08388	a	**FP**	E	WSXX	ZB(S)
08389	a	**B**	E	EWOC	OC	Wembley Yard
08393	a	**FE**	E	EWOC	OC	Dagenham Dock Up Sidings
08397	a	**0**	E	LWSP	CD	Padeswood Hall Cement Works
08401	a	**DG**	E	FDSI	IM	Immingham TMD
08402	a	**DG**	E	LWSP	CD	Allerton T&RSMD
08405	a	**DG**	E	FDSI	IM	Immingham TMD
08410	a	**DG**	GW	HJXX	PM	St. Philips Marsh T&RSMD
08411	a	**B**	E	LGML	ML	Motherwell TMD
08413	a	**DG**	E	WSXX	ZB(S)
08414	a	**0**	E	EWOC	OC	Euston Downside CARMD
08417	a	**B**	SO	CDJD	ZA(S)
08418	a	**F**	E	FDSD	DR	Doncaster TMD
08419	a	**B**	E	WSYX	ZC(S)
08428	a	**B**	E	WSXX	ZB(S)
08441	a	**B**	E	WSXX	ZB(S)

08442	a	F	E	FDSI	IM	*Immingham Yard*
08445	a	B	E	WSXX	ZB(S)	
08448	a	B	E	WSYX	BS(S)	
08449	a	B	E	WSYX	TT(S)	
08451		B	VW	HFSN	WN	*Willesden TMD*
08454		0	VW	HFSN	WN	*Willesden TMD*
08460	a	0	E	LWSP	CD	*Warrington Arpley Yards*
08466	a	F0	E	WSXX	ZB(S)	
08472	a	BR	RF	HBSH	EC	*Craigentinny T&RSMD*
08473	v	B	E	WSYX	LR(S)	
08480	a	G	E	EWEH	EH	*Eastleigh Yards*
08481		B	E	LNCF	CF	*Margam SD*
08482	a	DG	E	EWOC	OC	*Old Oak Common TMD*
08483	a	DG	GW	HJXX	PM	*St. Philips Marsh T&RSMD*
08484	a	DG	RC	KWSW	ZN	*Railcare, Wolverton*
08485	a	DG	E	LWSP	CD	*Warrington Arpley Yards*
08489	a	F	E	WSXX	WA(S)	
08492	a	B	E	WSXX	ZB(S)	
08493	a	B	E	LNCF	CF	*Margam SD*
08495		B	E	ENSN	TO	*Worksop Yards*
08499	a	F	E	FDSK	KY	*Knottingley T&RSMD*
08500		0	E	EWEH	EH	*Bristol Parkway*
08506	a	B	E	LNWF	CF	*Cardiff Canton TMD*
08509	a	F	E	FDSD	DR	*Tinsley Yard*
08510	a	B	E	FDSD	DR	*Doncaster TMD*
08511	a	R	E	ENSN	TO	*Toton TMD*
08512	a	F	E	FDSD	DR	*Doncaster TMD*
08514	a	B	E	FDSD	DR	*Doncaster TMD*
08515	a	B	E	WSYX	GD(S)	
08516	a	DG	E	ENSN	TO	*Peterborough SD*
08517	a	B	E	WSYX	SF(S)	
08519	a	0	E	WSXX	ZB(S)	
08523		ML	E	LBBS	BS	*Bescot TMD*
08525		F	MM	HISL	NL	*Neville Hill (InterCity) T&RSMD*
08526		E	E	EWOC	OC	*Hither Green TMD*
08527		0	AD	KCSI	ZI	*Adtranz, Ilford*
08528		DG	E	ENSN	TO	*Toton TMD*
08529		B	E	ENSN	TO	*Worksop Yards*
08530		DG	P	DFLS	OC	*Tilbury Container Terminal*
08531	a	DG	P	DFLS	OC	*Tilbury Container Terminal*
08534		DG	E	LGML	ML	*Motherwell TMD*
08535		DG	E	LBBS	BS	*Saltley SD*
08536		B	MM	HISE	DY(S)	
08538		DG	E	ENSN	TO	*Peterborough SD*
08540		DG	E	WSXX	ZB(S)	
08541		DG	E	EWOC	OC	*Temple Mills Yard*
08542		F	E	LBBS	BS	*Bescot TMD*
08543		DG	E	LBBS	BS	*Bescot Up Sidings*
08561		B	E	WSXX	ZB(S)	
08567		B	E	LBBS	BS	*Bescot TMD*
08568	a	B	RC	KGSS	ZH	*Railcare, Glasgow*

08569		E	E	ENSN	TO	*Toton TMD*
08571	a	B	RF	HBSH	EC	*Craigentinny T&RSMD*
08573		B	AD	KCSI	ZI	*Adtranz, Ilford*
08575		BR	P	DFLS	EH	*Southampton Maritime FLT*
08576		B	E	LNCF	CF	*Fowey Docks*
08577		B	E	FMSY	TE	*Tyne Yard*
08578		RG	E	LWSP	CD	*Blackburn Coal Concentration Depot*
08580		B	E	LBBS	BS	*Northampton*
08581		BR	E	WSYX	ZB(S)	
08582	a	DG	E	FMSY	TE	*Thornaby T&RSMD*
08585		B	P	DFLS	CD	*Crewe Basford Hall Yard*
08586	a	F	E	WSYX	AY(S)	
08587		B	E	FDSD	DR	*Doncaster TMD*
08588		BR	MM	HISL	NL	*Neville Hill (InterCity) T&RSMD*
08593		O	E	EWOC	OC	*Ipswich Upper yard*
08594		B	E	WSYX	TT(S)	
08597		B	E	FDSK	KY	*Knottingley T&RSMD*
08599		B	E	WSXX	AN(S)	
08601		O	E	EWEH	EH	*Allerton T&RSMD*
08605		B	E	FDSK	KY	*Hull King George Dock*
08607		B	E	WSYX	TT(S)	
08609		B	E	WSYX	ZB(S)	
08610		B	E	WSYX	ZB(S)	
08611		V	VW	HFSL	LO	*Longsight CARMD*
08616		O	CT	HGSS	TS	*Tyseley T&RSMD*
08617		O	VW	HFSN	WN	*Willesden TMD*
08618		B	E	WSYX	GD(S)	
08619		B	E	WSYX	ZB(S)	
08622		B	E	WSYX	ML(S)	
08623		B	E	LBBS	BS	*Bescot TMD*
08624		B	P	DFLS	ML	*Coatbridge FLT*
08625		B	E	WSYX	CF(S)	
08628		B	E	LBBS	BS	*Bescot TMD*
08629		RP	RC	KWSW	ZN	*Railcare, Wolverton*
08630		E	E	LGML	ML	*Deanside Transit, Hillingdon*
08631		FG	FG	SDFR	TM	*Birmingham Railway Museum, Tyseley*
08632		B	E	FDSI	IM	*Immingham Reception Sidings*
08633		RX	E	FMSY	TE	*Heaton T&RSMD*
08634		B	E	WSYX	SF(S)	
08635		B	E	EWOC	OC	*Temple Mills Yard*
08641		DG	GW	HJSL	LA	*Penzance*
08642		O	P	DFLS	CD	*Felixstowe North FLT*
08643		DG	GW	HJXX	PM	*St. Philips Marsh T&RSMD*
08644		IM	GW	HJSL	LA	*Laira T&RSMD*
08645		DG	GW	HJSL	LA	*Laira CS*
08646		F	E	EWEH	EH	*Eastleigh Yards*
08648		DG	GW	HJSL	LA	*Laira T&RSMD*
08649		O	AM	KESE	ZG	*Alstom, Eastleigh*
08651		DG	E	LNWK	CF	*Cardiff Canton TMD*
08653		FE	E	LWSP	CD	*Allerton T&RSMD*
08655		F	E	FDSK	KY	*Knottingley T&RSMD*

8661	a	F	E	WSYX	AN(S)	
8662		B	E	FDSK	KY	Goole Docks
8663	a	DG	GW	HJSL	LA	Plymouth Station
8664		B	E	EWEH	EH	Eastleigh Yards
8665		B	E	FDSI	IM	Immingham TMD
8666		B	E	WSYX	AN(S)	
8670	a	B	E	LGML	ML	Motherwell T&MD
8673		IM	E	WNZX	AN(S)	
8675		F	E	LGML	ML	Millerhill Yard
8676		B	E	FDSI	IM	Immingham TMD
8677		B	E	WSYX	ZB(S)	
8682		0	AD	KDSD	ZF	Adtranz, Doncaster
8683		B	E	LNWK	CF	Allied Steel & Wire, Cardiff
8685		B	E	LGML	ML	Polmadie T&RSMD
8689	a	0	E	FDSK	KY	Knottingley T&RSMD
8690		B	MM	HISE	DY	Derby Etches Park
8691		G	FL	DFLS	CD	Trafford Park FLT
8693		B	E	WSYX	ML(S)	
8694	a	B	E	EWOC	OC	Wembley Yard
8695	a	B	E	LWSP	CD	Crewe Gresty Lane Yard
8696	a	V	VW	HFSL	LO	Edge Hill CSD
8697	a	B	MM	HISE	DY	Derby Etches Park
8698	a	B	E	LBBS	BS	Bescot TMD
8700	a	B	E	WSYX	SF(S)	
8701	a	RX	E	LWSP	CD	Ince Moss
8702		B	E	WSXX	ZB(S)	
8703	a	B	E	LWSP	CD	Trafford Park RfD Terminal
8706		B	E	ENSN	TO	Toton TMD
8709		B	E	LGML	ML	Carlisle Currock T&RSMD
8711		RX	E	EWOC	OC	Acton Yard
8713	a	B	E	WSYX	ZB(S)	
8714		RX	E	ENSN	TO	Peterborough SD
8715	v	0	E	WSXX	SF(S)	
8718		B	E	WSYX	AY(S)	
8720	a	DG	E	LGML	ML	Motherwell TMD
8721		0	VW	HFSL	LO	Longsight Diesel T&RSMD
8723		B	E	WSYX	TT(S)	
8724		0	RF	MBDL	ZB	Foster Yeoman, Isle of Grain
8730		0	RC	KGSS	ZH	Railcare, Glasgow
8731		B	E	WSYX	ML(S)	
8733		B	E	WSYX	ML(S)	
8734		B	E	WSYX	CF(S)	
8735		DG	E	LGML	ML	Fort William
8737	a	FE	E	LWSP	CD	Warrington Arpley Yards
8738		E	E	LWSP	CD	Crewe Diesel Depot
8739		B	E	WSXX	AN(S)	
8740		F	E	WSXX	SF(S)	
8742		RX	E	LWSP	AN(S)	
8743		0	IC	MBDL	BH	ICI, Billingham
8745		FE	P	DFLS	CD	Felixstowe North FLT
8746		DG	E	LGML	ML	Killoch Disposal Point

08750	**B**	E	WSXX	SF(S)	
08751	**F**	E	WSXX	ZB(S)	
08752	**CE**	E	ENSN	TO	*Peterborough SD*
08754	**B**	SR	HASS	IS	*Inverness*
08755	**B**	E	WSYX	ZB(S)	
08756	**DG**	E	LNCF	CF	*Margam TMD*
08757	**RX**	E	WSXX	HT(S)	
08758	**B**	E	WSXX	SF(S)	
08762	**B**	SR	HASS	IS	*Inverness Yard*
08765	**DG**	E	LBBS	BS	*Rugby*
08768	**B**	E	LGML	ML	*Motherwell TMD*
08770 a	**DG**	E	LNCF	CF	*Margam TMD*
08773	**B**	E	WSXX	TO(S)	
08775	**E**	E	EWOC	OC	*Hither Green TMD*
08776 a	**DG**	E	ENSN	TO	*Toton TMD*
08780	**B**	GW	HJSE	LE	*Landore T&RSMD*
08782 a	**B**	E	FDSK	KY	*York Yard*
08783	**B**	E	FDSK	KY	*Hull King George Dock*
08784	**B**	E	WSXX	AN(S)	
08785 a	**O**	FL	DFLS	CD	*Crewe Basford Hall Yard*
08786 a	**DG**	E	LNCF	CF	*Tavistock Junction*
08790	**B**	VW	HFSL	LO	*Longsight Diesel T&RSMD*
08792	**B**	E	LNCF	CF	*Exeter St. Davids*
08793 a	**O**	E	WSYX	ZB(S)	
08795	**IM**	GW	HJSE	LE	*Landore T&RSMD*
08798	**B**	E	LNCF	CF	*Plymouth Station*
08799	**B**	E	EWOC	OC	*Stratford TMD*
08801	**B**	E	LNCF	CF	*Margam Yard*
08802	**RX**	E	LWSP	CD	*Dee Marsh Sidings*
08804	**B**	E	EWEH	EH	*Reading West Yard*
08805	**O**	CT	HGSS	TS	*Tyseley T&RSMD*
08806 a	**F**	E	FMSY	TE	*Tyne Yard*
08807	**BR**	E	LBBS	BS	*Bescot TMD*
08810 a	**B**	AR	HSSN	NC	*RFS(E), Doncaster*
08813 a	**DG**	E	FMSY	TE	*Thornaby T&RSMD*
08815	**B**	E	WSYX	AN(S)	
08817	**BR**	E	LWSP	CD	*Allerton T&RSMD*
08819	**DG**	E	LNWK	CF	*Allied Steel & Wire, Cardiff*
08822	**IM**	GW	HJSE	LE	*Landore T&RSMD*
08823 a	**B**	AD	KDSD	ZF	*Adtranz, Doncaster*
08824 a	**F**	E	FDSI	IM	*Scunthorpe Yard*
08825 a	**B**	E	EWOC	OC	*Dagenham Dock Up Sidings*
08826 a	**B**	E	WSYX	ML(S)	
08827 a	**B**	E	LGML	ML	*Motherwell TMD*
08828 a	**E**	E	LNWK	CF	*Allied Steel & Wire, Cardiff*
08829 a	**B**	E	WSYX	TT(S)	
08830	**G**	CA	HLSV	CF	*East Somerset Railway (on loan)*
08834	**FD**	RF	HBSH	ZB(S)	
08836	**I**	GW	HJXX	OO	*Old Oak Common HST Depot*
08837	**DG**	E	LWSP	CD	*Allerton T&RSMD*
08842	**B**	E	LWSP	CD	*Speke Junction Yard*

Increasing numbers of Class 08 are being repainted into EWS corporate red and gold livery. 08828 is seen here at Margam Yard on 28th January 1998.

Rodney Lissenden

BR 'general grey' liveried 09014 shunts type HAA coal hopper wagons at Milford West Sidings on 2nd October 1997.

John G. Teasdale

British Nuclear Fuels subsidiary Direct Rail Services is progressively taking over the haulage of nuclear flask trains from EWS. Here 20301 and 20302 wait at Lydd Town level crossing on the branch to Dungeness Power Station whilst on a crew

BR blue liveried 31434 pulls away from a signal check at Warrington Arpley with five salt hoppers forming a Runcorn–Arpley 'Enterprise' trip. The wagons are eventually destined for Dalry, in South West Scotland. **Nic Joynson**

▲ D6593 (33208) arrives at Ystrad Mynach with the 17.38 Rhymney–Cardiff Central service whilst on hire to Cardiff Railways on 30th April 1998.
Hugh Ballantyne

▼ 37153 (nearest camera) and 37154 carry the two different varieties of Transrail livery. They are seen here stabled at the erstwhile Stratford TMD on 30th May 1998.
Kevin Conkey

▲ Regional Railways liveried 37420 'The Scottish Hosteller' arrives at Holyhead with the 14.23 service from Birmingham New Street on 15th August 1998.

Nic Joynson

▼ 43101, complete with new style Virgin name 'The Irish Mail Trên Post Gwyddelig' heads on the 09.10 Aberdeen–Plymouth on 23rd September 1998. **Dave McAlone**

▲ Fragonset Railways' 47703 departs from Crewe with the 06.42 Poole–Liverpool Lime Street on 31st March 1998.   **Bob Swee**

▼ 47750 'Royal Mail Cheltenham' passes Barry Town with the all Rail Express Systems liveried 10.25 Bristol Temple Meads–Swansea empty van train on 2nd April 1998.   **Rodney Lissende**

Privately owned 50050 'Fearless' made its first outing on the main line journeying to Bournemouth TMD Open Day on 16th May 1998. It is one of only two preserved locos authorised for main line use at 90 mph. **Nic Joynson**

08844	B	E	WSXX	ZB(S)	
08847	B	AM	KESE	ZG	Alstom, Eastleigh
08853 a	B	RF	HBSH	BN	Bounds Green T&RSMD
08854	E	E	LNWK	CF	Cardiff Canton TMD
08855	B	E	WHZX	ZB(S)	
08856	B	E	EWEH	EH	Westbury
08865	B	E	EWOC	OC	Parkeston Yard
08866	B	E	LWSP	CD	Trafford Park RfD Terminal
08867	0	E	LWSP	CD	Brunner-Mond, Northwich
08868	B	HN	MBDL	CP	The Railway Age, Crewe
08869	G	AR	HSSN	NC(S)	
08870	0	HN	MBDL	NC	Norwich Crown Point T&RSMD
08872	DG	E	EWOC	OC	Three Bridges Engineers Yard
08873	RX	E	WSXX	ZB(S)	
08874	RF	MO	MBDL	ZB(S)	
08877	DG	E	FDSD	DR	Rotherham Steel Terminal
08879	0	E	WSXX	ZB(S)	
08880	B	E	WSXX	AN(S)	
08881	DG	E	LGML	ML	Falkland Yard
08882	B	E	LGML	ML	Motherwell TMD
08883	0	E	LGML	ML	Perth New Yard
08884	B	E	LBBS	BS	Saltley TMD
08886 †	E	E	WSTT	TO	Tyne Yard
08887 a	0	VW	HFSN	WN	Polmadie T&RSMD
08888	E	E	LBBS	BS	Bletchley T&RSMD
08890	DG	E	EWOC	OC	Wembley CSD
08891	B	P	DFLS	CD	Garston FLT
08892	GN	RF	HBSH	BN	Bounds Green T&RSMD
08893	DG	E	WSYX	ZB(S)	
08894	B	E	WSXX	AN(S)	
08895	B	E	WSYX	MW(S)	
08896	E	E	EWEH	EH	Bristol Barton Hill T&RSMD
08897	DG	E	LWSP	CD	Chester WRD
08899	MM	MM	HISE	DY	Derby Etches Park
08900	DG	E	LNWK	CF	Allied Steel & Wire, Cardiff
08901	B	E	WSYX	ZB(S)	
08902	B	E	WSXX	AN(S)	
08903	0	IC	MBDL	BH	ICI, Billingham
08904	B	E	EWEH	EH	Didcot Yard
08905	B	E	LBBS	BS	Saltley SD
08906	B	E	LGML	ML(S)	
08907	0	E	LWSP	CD	Longport Sidings
08908	B	MM	HISL	NL	Neville Hill (InterCity) T&RSMD
08909	ML	E	LBBS	BS	Bescot TMD
08910	B	E	LGML	ML	Aberdeen Guild Street Yard
08911	DG	E	LWSP	CD	Warrington Arpley Yards
08912	B	E	LGML	ML	Carlisle Currock T&RSMD
08913	DG	E	EWOC	OC	Stratford International Freight Terminal
08914	B	E	WSXX	ZB(S)	
08915	F	E	LWSP	CD	Peak Forest Sorting Sidings
08918	DG	E	WSXX	ZB(S)	

08919		**RX**	E	EWOC	OC	*Stoke Gifford Tip*
08920		**F**	E	LBBS	BS	*Wolverhampton Steel Terminal*
08921	†	**E**	E	WSTT	TO	*Wolverhampton Steel Terminal*
08922		**DG**	E	LGML	ML	*Carlisle Kingmoor Yard*
08924		**DG**	E	WSXX	ZB(S)	
08925		**B**	E	LWSP	CD	*Peak Forest Sorting Sidings*
08926		**DG**	E	WSXX	AN(S)	
08927		**B**	E	FDSI	IM	*Immingham TMD*
08928		**0**	AR	HSSN	NC(S)	
08931		**B**	E	WSYX	ZB(S)	
08932		**B**	E	LNWK	CF	*Allied Steel & Wire, Cardiff*
08933		**E**	E	WSXX	ZB(S)	
08934	a	**0**	VW	HFSN	WN	*Willesden TMD*
08938		**0**	E	WSYX	ML(S)	
08939		**B**	E	LWSP	CD	*Crewe International Electric Depot*
08940		**B**	E	WSYX	AN(S)	
08941		**B**	E	LNCF	CF	*St. Blazey T&RSMD*
08942		**B**	E	WSXX	ZB(S)	
08944		**DG**	E	WSXX	ZB(S)	
08946		**FE**	E	LBBS	BS	*Saltley SD*
08947		**B**	E	EWEH	EH	*Bristol Barton Hill T&RSMD*
08948	c	**EU**	EU	GPSS	OC	*North Pole International T&RSMD*
08950		**IM**	MM	HISL	NL	*Neville Hill (InterCity) T&RSMD*
08951		**DG**	E	WSXX	ZB(S)	
08952		**B**	E	WSYX	ML(S)	
08953		**DG**	E	LNCF	CF	*St. Blazey T&RSMD*
08954		**F**	E	WSXX	ZB(S)	
08955		**T**	E	LNWK	CF	*Allied Steel & Wire, Cardiff*
08956		**B**	SO	CDJD	DY	*Railway Technical Centre, Derby*
08957		**E**	E	LNWK	CF	*Newport Godfrey Road*
08958		**B**	E	WSXX	SF(S)	

Class 08/9. Reduced height cab. Details as Class 08/0 except:
Converted: 1985–87 by BR at Landore depot.
Dimensions: 8.92 x 2.59 x 3.60 m.

08993		**T**	E	LNCF	CF	*Margam Yard*
08994	a	**FR**	E	ENSN	TO	*Toton Yard*
08995	a	**T**	E	FMSY	TE	*Boulby Mine*

Names:

08578	Lybert Dickinson
08629	BRML WOLVERTON LEVEL 5
08649	G.H. Stratton
08661	Europa
08682	Lionheart
08701	The Sorter
08711	EAGLE C.U.R.C.
08714	Cambridge
08743	ANGIE
08790	M.A. SMITH

08869	The Canary
08879	Sheffield Childrens Hospital
08888	Postman's Pride
08896	STEPHEN DENT
08919	Steep Holm
08950	Neville Hill 1st
08993	ASHBURNHAM
08994	GWENDRAETH
08995	KIDWELLY

CLASS 09   BR/ENGLISH ELECTRIC   0–6–0

Built: 1959–62 by BR at Darlington or Horwich Works.
Engine: English Electric 6KT of 298 kW (400 hp) at 680 rpm.
Main Generator: English Electric 801.
Traction Motors: English Electric 506.
Max. Tractive Effort: 111 kN (25000 lbf).
Cont. Tractive Effort: 39 kN (8800 lbf) at 11.6 mph.
Power At Rail: 201 kW (269 hp).   **Train Brakes:** Air & vacuum.
Brake Force: 19 t.   **Dimensions:** 8.92 x 2.59 x 3.89 m.
Weight: 50 t.   **Wheel Diameter:** 1372 mm.
Design Speed: 27 mph.   **Max. Speed:** 27 mph.
Fuel Capacity: 3037 litres.   **RA:** 5.
Train Supply: Not equipped.   **Multiple Working:** Not equipped.
Note: 09017 was renumbered from 97806 during 1998.
Non-standard livery/numbering:
- 09017 is as **B**, but with a grey cab.

Class 09/0. Standard Design.

09001	**B**	E	LNCF	CF	*Margam TMD*
09003	**B**	E	LNCF	CF	*Cardiff Canton TMD*
09004	**B**	SC	HWSU	SU(S)	
09005	**DG**	E	FDSK	KY	*Healey Mills Yard*
09006	**ML**	E	EWOC	OC	*Hither Green TMD*
09007	**ML**	E	FDSD	DR	*Tinsley Yard*
09008	**DG**	E	LNCF	CF	*St. Blazey T&RSMD*
09009	**E**	E	EWOC	OC	*Co-Steel, Sheerness*
09010	**DG**	E	EWOC	OC	*Parkeston Yard*
09011	**DG**	E	EWOC	OC	*Hoo Junction*
09012	**DG**	E	EWOC	OC	*Wembley Yard*
09013	**DG**	E	LNCF	CF	*Tavistock Junction*
09014	**DG**	E	FDSD	DR	*Doncaster TMD*
09015	**DG**	E	LNCF	CF	*Barry WRD*
09016	**DG**	E	EWEH	EH	*Eastleigh Yards*
09017	**0**	E	LNCF	CF	*Sudbrook Pumping Station*
09018	**ML**	E	EWOC	OC	*Old Oak Common TMD*
09019	**ML**	E	EWOC	OC	*Stewarts Lane T&RSMD*
09020	**B**	E	WSXX	ZB(S)	
09021	**FE**	E	LBBS	BS	*Saltley TMD*
09022	**B**	E	WSXX	AN(S)	
09023	**ML**	E	LWSP	CD	*Allerton T&RSMD*
09024	**ML**	E	EWOC	OC	*Hoo Junction*
09025	**B**	SC	HWSU	SU	*Brighton Lovers Walk EMU Depot*
09026	**G**	SC	HWSU	SU	*Brighton Lovers Walk EMU Depot*

Names:

09009	Three Bridges C.E.D.	09026	William Pearson
09012	Dick Hardy		

Class 09/1. Converted from Class 08/0. 110 V electrical equipment. Details as Class 09/0 except:
Built: 1960–61 by BR at Crewe, Derby or Horwich Works. Converted 1992–93 by RFS Industries, Kilnhurst.

09101	**DG**	E	EWEH	EH	*Swindon Cocklebury Yard*
09102	**DG**	E	EWEH	EH	*Wembley Yard*
09103	**DG**	E	LGML	ML	*Motherwell TMD*
09104	**DG**	E	LGML	ML	*Mossend Yard*
09105	**DG**	E	LNCF	CF	*Newport Alexandra Dock Junction*
09106	**DG**	E	FMSY	TE	*Thornaby T&RSMD*
09107	**DG**	E	LNCF	CF	*Newport Alexandra Dock Junction*

Class 09/2. Converted from Class 08/0. 90 V electrical equipment. Details as Class 09/0 except:
Built: 1958–60 by BR at Crewe or Derby Works. Converted 1992 by RFS Industries, Kilnhurst.

09201	a	**DG**	E	FDSK	KY	*Knottingley T&RSMD*
09202		**DG**	E	LGML	ML	*Aberdeen Guild Street Yard*
09203		**DG**	E	LNCF	CF	*Cardiff Canton TMD*
09204		**DG**	E	FMSY	TE	*Thornaby T&RSMD*
09205		**DG**	E	LGML	ML	*Millerhill Yard*

CLASS 20   ENGLISH ELECTRIC   Bo–Bo

Built: 1957–68 by English Electric Company at Vulcan Foundry, Newton le Willows or by Robert Stephenson & Hawthorn at Darlington.
Engine: English Electric 8SVT Mk. II of 746 kW (1000 hp) at 850 rpm.
Main Generator: English Electric 819/3C.
Traction Motors: English Electric 526/5D or 526/8D.
Max. Tractive Effort: 187 kN (42000 lbf).
Cont. Tractive Effort: 111 kN (25000 lbf) at 11 mph.

Power At Rail: 574 kW (770 hp).	**Train Brakes:** Air & vacuum.
Brake Force: 35 t.	**Dimensions:** 14.25 x 2.67 x 3.86 m.
Weight: 73.4–73.5 t.	**Wheel Diameter:** 1092 mm.
Design Speed: 75mph.	**Max. Speed:** 60 mph.
Fuel Capacity: 1727 litres.	**RA:** 5.
Train Supply: Not equipped.	**Multiple Working:** Blue Star.

Non-standard livery/numbering:
• 20092/169 are in British Railways Board Central Services livery of red and grey.

Class 20/0. Standard Design.

20007	s	**B**	DR	XHSS	ZB(S)
20016	s	**B**	E	WNZX	BS(S)
20032	s	**B**	DR	XHSS	ZB(S)
20057	s	**B**	E	WNZX	BS(S)
20059	s	**FR**	E	WNXX	MW(S)
20066		**B**	E	WNZX	BS(S)
20072	s	**B**	DR	XHSS	ZB(S)
20073	s	**B**	E	WHZX	BS(S)
20081	s	**B**	E	WNZX	BS(S)

0087	s	**BR**	E	WNZX	BS(S)	
0088	s	**RF**	DR	XHSS	SD(S)	
0092		**0**	E	WNZX	BS(S)	
0105	s	**RF**	DR	XHSS	ZB(S)	
0118		**FR**	E	WNZX	BS(S)	
0119		**B**	E	WNZX	TT(S)	
0121	s	**B**	DR	XHSS	ZB(S)	
0132	s	**FR**	E	WNZX	BS(S)	
0138		**FR**	E	WNZX	BS(S)	
0145		**RF**	DR	XHSS	ZB(S)	
0154	s	**B**	E	WNZX	TT(S)	
0159	s	**RF**	DR	XHSS	ZB(S)	
0165		**FR**	E	WNZX	BS(S)	
0168	s	**B**	E	WNZX	MW(S)	
0169	s	**0**	E	WNZX	BS(S)	
0177	s	**B**	E	WNZX	TT(S)	
0209	s	**B**	DR	XHSS	ZK(S)	
0215	s	**FR**	DR	XHSS	ZB(S)	

Class 20/3. Direct Rail Services refurbished locos. Details as Class 20/0 except:
Refurbished: 1995–96 by Brush Traction at Loughborough (20301–305) or 997–99 by RFS(E) at Doncaster (20306–315).
Train Brakes: Air.   **Max. Speed:** 75 mph.
Brake Force: 31 t.   **Fuel Capacity:** 4727 litres.
Multiple Working: DRS System (20301–305 at nose end only).

0301		**DR**	DR	XHSD	SD	FURNESS RAILWAY 150
0302		**DR**	DR	XHSD	SD	
0303		**DR**	DR	XHSD	SD	
0304		**DR**	DR	XHSD	SD	
0305		**DR**	DR	XHSD	SD	
0306	(20131)	**DR**	DR	XHSD	SD	
0307	(20128)	**DR**	DR	XHSD	SD	
0308	(20187)	**DR**	DR	XHSD	SD	
0309	(20075)	**DR**	DR	XHSD	SD	
0310	(20190)	**DR**	DR	XHSD	SD	
0311	(20102)	**DR**	DR	XHSD	SD	
0312	(20042)	**DR**	DR	XHSD	SD	
0313	(20194)	**DR**	DR	XHSD	SD	
0314	(20104)	**DR**	DR	XHSD	SD	
0315	(20117)	**DR**	DR	XHSS	ZB(S)	

Class 20/9. Direct Rail Services (former Hunslet-Barclay) refurbished locos.
Details as Class 20/0 except:
Refurbished: 1989 by Hunslet-Barclay at Kilmarnock.
Train Brakes: Air.   **Fuel Capacity:** 1727 (+ 4727) litres.

20901		**HB**	DR	XHSS	SD(S)
20902	+	**HB**	DR	XHSS	SD(S)
20903	+	**HB**	DR	XHSS	KD(S)
20904		**HB**	DR	XHSS	KD(S)
20905	+	**HB**	DR	XHSS	KD(S)
20906		**HB**	DR	XHSS	KD(S)

CLASS 31   BRUSH/ENGLISH ELECTRIC   A1A–A1A

Built: 1958–62 by Brush Traction at Loughborough.
Engine: English Electric 12SVT of 1100 kW (1470 hp) at 850 rpm.
Main Generator: Brush TG160-48.
Traction Motors: Brush TM73-68.
Max. Tractive Effort: 160 or * 190 kN (35900 or * 42800 lbf).
Cont. TE: 83 kN (18700 lbf) at 23.5 mph. (* 99 kN (22250 lbf) at 19.7 mph.).
Power At Rail: 872 kW (1170 hp).   **Train Brakes:** Air & vacuum.
Brake Force: 49 t.   **Dimensions:** 17.30 x 2.67 x 3.87 m.
Weight: 106.7–111 t.   **Wheel Diameter:** 1092/1003 mm.
Design Speed: 90 (* 80) mph.   **Max. Speed:** 60 mph.
Fuel Capacity: 2409 litres.   **RA:** 5 or 6.
Train Supply: Not equipped.   **Multiple Working:** Blue Star.
Note: 31452 was renumbered from 31552 during 1998.
Non-standard livery/numbering:
•   31116 is grey and yellow with red stripes.

Class 31/1. Standard Design. Details as above except: RA: 5.

31102		CE	E	WNYX	CD(S)
31105	*	T	E	WNZX	BS(S)
31106	*	CE	E	WNZX	BS(S)
31107		CE	E	WNZX	BS(S)
31110		CE	E	WMAN	BS
31112	*	TC	E	WNXX	BS(S)
31113		CE	E	WMAN	BS
31116		0	E	WNZX	TU(S)
31119		CE	E	WNXX	CL(S)
31125		CE	E	WNZX	BS(S)
31126		CE	E	WNYX	SP(S)
31128		FO	E	WNZX	BS(S)
31130		FC	E	WNZX	BS(S)
31132		FO	E	WNXX	BS(S)
31134		CE	E	WNYX	BS(S)
31135		CE	E	WNZX	TU(S)
31142		CE	E	WMAN	BS
31144		CE	E	WNXX	CL(S)
31145	r	CE	E	WNYX	SP(S)
31146	r	CE	E	WNYX	BS(S)	Brush Veteran
31147		CE	E	WNZX	BS(S)
31149		FR	E	WNYX	TT(S)
31154		CE	E	WMAN	BS
31155		FA	E	WNZX	BS(S)
31158		CE	E	WNZX	BS(S)
31160		F	E	WNYX	SP(S)
31163		CE	E	WMAN	BS
31164		FO	E	WNZX	BS(S)
31166	r	CE	E	WMAN	BS
31168		B	E	WNZX	BS(S)
31171		FO	E	WNZX	BS(S)

31174	**CE**	E	WNZX	BS(S)	
31178	**CE**	E	WNZX	BS(S)	
31180	**FR**	E	WNZX	TU(S)	
31181	**CE**	E	WNZX	TU(S)	
31184	**FO**	E	WNZX	TU(S)	
31185	**CE**	E	WNZX	BS(S)	
31186	**CE**	FG	SDFR	TM(S)	
31187	**CE**	E	WNZX	TU(S)	
31188	**CE**	E	WMAN	BS	
31190	**CE**	E	WMAN	BS	
31191	**CE**	FG	SDFR	TM(S)	
31196	**CE**	E	WNZX	SF(S)	
31199	**FC**	E	WNYX	TT(S)	
31200	**FC**	E	WNYX	BA(S)	
31201	**FC**	E	WMAN	BS	
31203	**CE**	E	WMAN	BS	
31205	**FR**	E	WNZX	TU(S)	
31206	**CE**	E	WNXX	BS(S)	
31207	**CE**	E	WMAN	BS	
31209	**FA**	E	WNZX	TU(S)	
31219	**CE**	E	WNZX	TU(S)	
31224	**CE**	E	WNXX	CL(S)	
31229	**CE**	E	WNZX	BS(S)	
31230 *	**FO**	E	WNZX	TU(S)	
31232	**CE**	E	WNZX	BS(S)	
31233	**CE**	E	WMAN	BS	Severn Valley Railway
31235	**CE**	E	WNXX	CL(S)	
31237	**CE**	E	WNZX	BS(S)	
31238	**CE**	E	WNYX	SP(S)	
31242	**CE**	E	WMAN	BS	
31247	**FR**	E	WNZX	TU(S)	
31248	**FO**	E	WNZX	BS(S)	
31250	**CE**	E	WNZX	TU(S)	
31252	**FO**	E	WNYX	PB(S)	
31255	**CE**	E	WMAN	BS	
31263	**CE**	E	WNZX	BS(S)	
31268	**CE**	E	WNZX	TU(S)	
31270	**F**	E	WNXX	CL(S)	
31273	**CE**	E	WNYX	BS(S)	
31276	**FC**	E	WNZX	TU(S)	
31282	**FR**	E	WNZX	BS(S)	
31283	**B**	E	WNZX	SF(S)	
31285	**CE**	E	WNXX	CL(S)	
31286	**B**	E	WNZX	BS(S)	
31289	**B**	E	WNZX	BS(S)	
31290	**CE**	E	WNZX	TU(S)	
31294	**FA**	E	WNZX	TU(S)	
31296	**FA**	E	WHZX	CP(S)	
31299	**FO**	E	WNZX	SF(S)	
31301	**FR**	E	WNZX	BS(S)	
31302	**FP**	E	WNYX	SP(S)	

31304	**FC**	E	WNYX	SP(S)	
31306	**CE**	E	WMAN	BS	
31308	**CE**	E	WMAN	BS	
31312	**FC**	E	WNYX	SP(S)	
31317	**FO**	E	WNZX	BS(S)	
31319	**FC**	E	WNYX	BS(S)	
31320	**B**	E	WNZX	SF(S)	
31327	**FR**	E	WNXX	CL(S)	

Class 31/4. Electric Train Supply equipment. Details as Class 31/1 except:
Max. Speed: 90 mph.   **RA:** 6.
Train Supply: Electric, but not operational (e – Electric, index 66).

31402		**B**	E	WNZX	BS(S)	
31403		**B**	E	WNZX	TU(S)	
31405		**IM**	E	WNXX	ZF(S)	Mappa Mundi
31407		**ML**	E	WNZX	BS(S)	
31408		**B**	E	WNYX	SP(S)	
31411		**DG**	E	WNZX	BS(S)	
31415		**B**	E	WNZX	BS(S)	
31417		**DG**	E	WNZX	BS(S)	
31420	e	**IM**	E	WMAN	BS	
31421		**RR**	E	WNYX	BA(S)	
31422		**IM**	E	WNXX	BS(S)	
31423		**IM**	E	WNZX	BS(S)	
31427		**B**	E	WMAN	BS	
31428		**B**	E	WNZX	BS(S)	
31432		**B**	E	WNYX	SP(S)	
31434		**B**	E	WNYX	BS(S)	
31435		**CE**	E	WNZX	BS(S)	
31439		**RR**	E	WNXX	BS(S)	North Yorkshire Moors Railway
31442		**B**	E	WNYX	BA(S)	
31444		**CE**	E	WNYX	SP(S)	
31450		**B**	E	WMAN	BS	
31452	e	**FG**	FG	SDFR	TM	
31455		**RR**	E	WNYX	SP(S)	
31459		**B**	FG	SDFR	TM(S)	
31460		**B**	E	WNZX	BS(S)	
31461		**DG**	FG	SDFR	TM(S)	
31462		**DG**	E	WNZX	BS(S)	
31465	e	**RR**	E	WMAN	BS	
31466	e	**E**	E	WMAN	BS	
31467		**B**	E	WNZX	BS(S)	
31468	e	**FG**	FG	SDFR	TM	

Class 31/1 ("31/5"). Electric Train Supply equipment fitted, but isolated. Details as Class 31/1 except: **RA:** 6.
Max. Speed: 60 mph.   **Train Supply:** Electric, isolated.

31512	**CE**	E	WNZX	BS(S)	
31514	**CE**	E	WMAN	BS	
31516	**CE**	E	WNZX	BS(S)	
31519	**CE**	E	WNYX	SP(S)	

31524	CE	E	WNZX	BS(S)
31526	CE	E	WNZX	BS(S)
31530	CE	E	WMAN	BS
31531	CE	E	WNZX	TU(S)
31533	CE	E	WNZX	BS(S)
31537	CE	E	WNXX	BS(S)
31538	B	E	WNXX	CL(S)
31541	CE	E	WNYX	OC(S)
31545	B	E	WNZX	BS(S)
31546	CE	E	WNZX	BS(S)
31547	CE	E	WNZX	TU(S)
31548	CE	E	WNZX	BS(S)
31549	CE	FG	SDFR	TM(S)
31553	CE	E	WNZX	TU(S)
31554	CE	E	WMAN	BS
31556	CE	E	WNXX	CL(S)
31558	CE	FG	`SDFR	TM(S)
31569	CE	E	WNZX	TU(S)

CLASS 33   BRCW/SULZER   Bo–Bo

Built: 1960–62 by the Birmingham Railway Carriage & Wagon Company at Smethwick.
Engine: Sulzer 8LDA28 of 1160 kW (1550 hp) at 750 rpm.
Main Generator: Crompton Parkinson CG391B1.
Traction Motors: Crompton Parkinson C171C2.
Max. Tractive Effort: 200 kN (45000 lbf).
Cont. Tractive Effort: 116 kN (26000 lbf) at 17.5 mph.
Power At Rail: 906 kW (1215 hp).   **Train Brakes:** Air & vacuum.
Brake Force: 35 t.   **Dimensions:** 15.47 x 2.82 x 3.86 m.
Weight: 77.7 t.   **Wheel Diameter:** 1092 mm.
Design Speed: 85 mph.   **Max. Speed:** 60 (* 75, † 85) mph.
Fuel Capacity: 3410 litres.   **RA:** 6.
Train Supply: Electric, not operational (e – index 48 (750 V dc only).
Multiple Working: Blue Star.
Non-standard livery/numbering:
- 33012 carries number 6515.
- 33051 also carries number 6569.
- 33116 also carries number D6535.
- 33208 carries number D6593.

Class 33/0. Standard Design.

33012	e†	B	71	MBDL	RL	
33019		CE	E	WLAN	EH	
33021	e†	R	FG	SDFR	TM	Eastleigh
33025		CE	E	WLAN	EH	
33026		CE	E	WNXX	EH(S)	
33030	†	E	E	WLAN	EH	
33038		B	E	WNZX	SF(S)	
33046		CE	E	WNZX	EH(S)	
33051		B	E	WNXX	EH(S)	Shakespeare Cliff

Class 33/1. Buckeye Couplings and SR Multiple Working Equipment. Details as Class 33/0 except:
Train Brakes: Air, vacuum & electro-pneumatic.
Weight: 78.5 t.   **Multiple Working:** Blue Star & SR System.

33103	e†	**G**	CM	CTLO	TM
33109	e	**B**	71	MBDL	RL
33116		**B**	E	WNXX	OC(S)

Class 33/2. Narrow body profile. Details as Class 33/0 except:
Weight: 77.5 t.   **Dimensions:** 15.47 x 2.64 x 3.86 m.

33202		**CE**	E	WLAN	EH
33205		**FD**	E	WNZX	OC(S)
33208	e*	**G**	71	MBDL	RL

CLASS 37   ENGLISH ELECTRIC TYPE 3   Co–Co

Built: 1960–65 by English Electric Company at Vulcan Foundry, Newton le Willows or by Robert Stephenson & Hawthorn at Darlington.
Engine: English Electric 12CSVT of 1300 kW (1750 hp) at 850 rpm.
Main Generator: English Electric 822/10G.
Traction Motors: English Electric 538/A.
Max. Tractive Effort: 245 kN (55500 lbf).
Cont. Tractive Effort: 156 kN (35000 lbf) at 13.6 mph.
Power At Rail: 932 kW (1250 hp).   **Train Brakes:** Air & vacuum.
Brake Force: 50 t.   **Dimensions:** 18.75 x 2.74 x 3.94 or 3.99 m.
Weight: 102.8–108.4 t.   **Wheel Diameter:** 1092 mm.
Design Speed: 90 mph.   **Max. Speed:** 80 mph.
Fuel Capacity: 4046 (+ 7678) litres.   **RA:** 5.
Train Supply: Not equipped.   **Multiple Working:** Blue Star.
Notes: 37072–074/131–298/358/370–384 have roof mounted horns and are 3.99 m. high. Others have nose mounted horns and are 3.94 m. high.
Non-standard liveries/numbering:
• 37104 is officially numbered 37345, but it is doubtful it has ever carried this number.
• 37116 is as **B**, but with Transrail markings.
• 37350 also carries number D6700.
• 37403 carries number D6607.

Class 37/0. Standard Design. Details as above.

37010		**CE**	E	WKBN	TO
37012	§	**CE**	E	WKMS	TO
37013	+	**ML**	E	WKBN	TO
37019	+	**FD**	E	WNYX	HM(S)
37023	ř	**ML**	E	WKMB	ML	Stratford TMD Quality Approved
37025		**BL**	E	WKBN	TO	Inverness TMD
37026	+	**FD**	E	WNYX	SP(S)
37037		**F**	E	WKBN	TO
37038		**CE**	E	WKBN	TO
37040		**E**	E	WKBN	TO
37042	+	**E**	E	WKBN	TO

37043	r§	TC	E	WKMB	ML	
37045	+	F	E	WNYX	TT(S)	
37046		CE	E	WKBN	TO	
37047	+	ML	E	WKBN	TO	
37048		MG	E	WNYX	TT(S)	
37051		E	E	WKBN	TO	Merehead
37054		CE	E	WKBN	TO	
37055	+	ML	E	WKBN	TO	
37057	+	E	E	WKBN	TO	Viking
37058	+	CE	E	WKBN	TO	
37059	+	FD	E	WKBN	TO	
37063	a+	FD	E	WNYX	ZB(S)	
37065	+	ML	E	WKBN	TO	
37068	+	FD	E	WNYX	IM(S)	
37069	+	CE	E	WKBN	TO	
37071	+	CE	E	WKBN	TO	
37072	+	DG	E	WNYX	ZB(S)	
37073	+	T	E	WKBN	TO	Fort William/An Gearasdan
37074	+	ML	E	WKBN	TO	
37075	+	F	E	WNXX	IM(S)	
37077		ML	E	WKBN	TO	
37078	+	FM	E	WNYX	ML(S)	
37079	+	FD	E	WNYX	ZH(S)	Medite
37083	+	CE	E	WNYX	DR(S)	
37087		CE	E	WNXX	BA(S)	
37088		TC	E	WNYX	ML(S)	Clydesdale
37092		CE	E	WNYX	TT(S)	
37095	+	CE	E	WNYX	ZB(S)	
37097		CE	E	WNYX	MH(S)	
37098	+	CE	E	WNYX	OC(S)	
37100	+	T	E	WKBN	TO	
37101	+	FD	E	WHZX	IM(S)	
37104		CE	E	WNYX	IM(S)	
37106	+	CE	E	WKBN	TO	
37107	+	FD	E	WNYX	SP(S)	
37108	+	F	E	WNYX	BS(S)	
37109	a	E	E	WKBN	TO	
37110	+	F	E	WNYX	IM(S)	
37114	r+	E	E	WKMB	ML	City of Worcester
37116	r+	0	E	WKMB	ML	Sister Dora
37131	+	F	E	WKBN	TO	
37133	a§	CE	E	WKMS	TO	
37137		MG	E	WNYX	TT(S)	
37139	+	FC	E	WNYX	TE(S)	
37140		CE	E	WKBN	TO	
37141		CE	E	WNYX	ZC(S)	
37142		CE	E	WNYX	BA(S)	
37144	r	FA	E	WNYX	IM(S)	
37146		CE	E	WKBN	TO	
37152	r§	IS	E	WKMB	ML	
37153	r§	TC	E	WKMB	ML	

37154	+§	T	E	WKMS	TO	
37156		T	E	WKBN	TO	
37158		CE	E	WKBN	TO	
37162	+	DG	E	WKBN	TO	
37165	r+	TC	E	WKMB	ML	
37170	r	TC	E	WKMB	ML	
37174	a	E	E	WKBN	TO	
37175	a	CE	E	WKBN	TO	
37178	+§	F	E	WKMS	TO	
37184	§	CE	E	WNYX	BS(S)	
37185	+	CE	E	WKBN	TO	Lea & Perrins
37188		TC	E	WNYX	TT(S)	
37191	a§	CE	E	WKMS	TO	
37194	+	MG	E	WKBN	TO	British International Freight Association
37196	§	CE	E	WKMS	TO	
37197	+§	TC	E	WKMS	TO	
37198	+	ML	E	WKBN	TO	
37201		TC	E	WNXX	BS(S)	
37203		ML	E	WKBN	TO	
37207		CE	E	WNXX	BS(S)	
37209		BL	E	WNYX	DR(S)	
37211		CE	E	WKBN	TO	
37212	+	T	E	WKBN	TO	
37213	+	FC	E	WNYX	TT(S)	
37214	+	T	E	WNXX	BS(S)	
37216	r+	ML	E	WKBN	TO	
37217	+	B	E	WNXX	AY(S)	
37218	+	F	E	WNXX	IM(S)	
37219		ML	E	WKBN	TO	
37220	r+	E	E	WKMB	ML	
37221	r	T	E	WKMB	ML	
37222	+	MG	E	WNYX	CF(S)	
37223	+	FC	E	WNXX	IM(S)	
37225	+	F	E	WKBN	TO	
37227	+	MG	E	WNYX	SL(S)	
37229	+§	FC	E	WKMS	TO	
37230	+§	TC	E	WKMS	TO	
37232	r§	TC	E	WNXX	ML(S)	The Institution of Railway Signal Engineers
37235	+	F	E	WNYX	DR(S)	
37238	+	F	E	WKBN	TO	
37240	+	CE	E	WNXX	BS(S)	
37241		MG	E	WNYX	TT(S)	
37242	+	ML	E	WKBN	TO	
37244	+	F	E	WKBN	TO	
37245		CE	E	WKBN	TO	
37248	+	ML	E	WKBN	TO	Midland Railway Centre
37250	+	T	E	WKBN	TO	
37251	a+	IS	E	WNYX	ML(S)	The Northern Lights[1]
37252		FD	E	WNYX	DR(S)	

37254	+	**CE**	E	WNYX	ZH(S)	
37255	+§	**CE**	E	WKMS	TO	
37261	a+	**FD**	E	WKBN	TO	Caithness
37262	+§	**DG**	E	WKMS	TO	Dounreay[1]
37263	§	**CE**	E	WKMS	TO	
37264		**CE**	E	WKBN	TO	
37274	+	**ML**	E	WKBN	TO	
37275	+§	**B**	E	WKMS	TO	Oor Wullie
37278	+	**FC**	E	WNYX	TT(S)	
37293	+	**ML**	E	WKBN	TO	
37294	r+	**CE**	E	WKMB	ML	
37298		**E**	E	WKBN	TO	

Class 37/3. Re-geared (CP7) bogies. Details as Class 37/0 except:
Max. Tractive Effort: 250 kN (56180 lbf).
Cont. Tractive Effort: 184 kN (41250 lbf) at 11.4 mph.
Design Speed: 80 mph.   **Max. Speed:** 80 mph.
Notes: 37334 is mounted on standard bogies, but has not been renumbered back to Class 37/0. 37384 was renumbered from 37258 during 1998.

37330	+§	**BL**	E	WNYX	TT(S)	
37331		**FM**	E	WNYX	DR(S)	
37332	+§	**FC**	E	WKMS	TO	The Coal Merchants' Association of Scotland[1]
37334	a+§	**F**	E	WNXX	IM(S)	
37335	+	**F**	E	WNYX	IM(S)	
37340	+	**FD**	E	WNYX	IM(S)	
37341	+	**F**	E	WNYX	TE(S)	
37343		**CE**	E	WNYX	TT(S)	
37344	+	**FD**	E	WNYX	IM(S)	
37350	+	**G**	E	WKBN	TO	NATIONAL RAILWAY MUSEUM
37351	+	**TC**	E	WKBN	TO	
37358	+	**F**	E	WNXX	IM(S)	
37359		**FP**	E	WNYX	TE(S)	
37370		**E**	E	WKBN	TO	
37371	+	**ML**	E	WKBN	TO	
37372		**ML**	E	WKBN	TO	
37375	+	**ML**	E	WKBN	TO	
37376	+	**F**	E	WKBN	TO	
37377	+	**CE**	E	WKBN	TO	
37379	r	**ML**	E	WKBN	TO	Ipswich WRD Quality Approved
37380		**MG**	E	WKBN	TO	
37381	+	**FD**	E	WNYX	FH(S)	
37382		**FP**	E	WNYX	IM(S)	
37383	+	**ML**	E	WKBN	TO	
37384	+§	**CE**	E	WKMS	TO	

Class 37/4. Refurbished locos with train supply equipment. Main generator replaced by alternator. Re-geared (CP7) bogies. Details as class 37/0 except:
Main Alternator: Brush BA1005A.
Max. Tractive Effort: 256 kN (57440 lbf).
Cont. Tractive Effort: 184 kN (41250 lbf) at 11.4 mph.

Power At Rail: 935 kW (1254 hp).
Dimensions: 18.75 x 2.74 x 3.99 m.   **Weight:** 107 t.
Design Speed: 80 mph.   **Max. Speed:** 80 mph.
Fuel Capacity: 7678 litres.   **Train Supply:** Electric, index 38.

37401	r	E	E	WKCD	CD	Mary Queen of Scots
37402		F	E	WKCN	IM	Bont Y Bermo
37403	r	G	E	WKMB	TO	Ben Cruachan
37404	r	T	E	WKMB	ML	Loch Long
37405	r	E	E	WKMB	ML	
37406	r	T	E	WKMB	ML	The Saltire Society
37407		T	E	WKCN	IM	Blackpool Tower
37408		E	E	WKCN	IM	Loch Rannoch
37409	r	T	E	WKMB	ML	Loch Awe
37410	r	T	E	WKMB	ML	Aluminium 100
37411		E	E	WKCN	CF	Ty Hafan
37412		T	E	WKCN	CF	Driver John Elliott
37413	r	E	E	WKMB	ML	The Scottish Railway Preservation Society
37414		RR	E	WKCD	CD	Cathays C & W Works 1846-1993
37415		E	E	WKCD	CD	
37416		E	E	WKCN	CF	
37417		E	E	WKCN	IM	RAIL Magazine
37418		E	E	WKCD	CD	East Lancashire Railway
37419		E	E	WKCN	CF	
37420		RR	E	WKCD	CD	The Scottish Hosteller
37421		E	E	WKCD	CD	
37422		RR	E	WKCD	CD	Robert F. Fairlie Locomotive Engineer 1831-1885
37423	r	T	E	WKMB	TO	Sir Murray Morrison 1873–1948 Pioneer of the British Aluminium Industry
37424	r	T	E	WKMB	ML	
37425		RR	E	WKCN	ML	Sir Robert McAlpine/Concrete Bob
37426		E	E	WKCD	CD	
37427		E	E	WKCN	ML	
37428	r	GS	E	WKMB	ML	
37429		RR	E	WKCN	IM	Eisteddfod Genedlaethol
37430	r	T	E	WKMB	ML	Cwmbrân
37431		IM	E	WKCN	TO	

Class 37/5. Refurbished locos without train supply equipment. Main generator replaced by alternator. Re-geared (CP7) bogies. Details as class 37/4 except:
Max. Tractive Effort: 248 kN (55590 lbf).
Dimensions: 18.75 x 2.74 x 3.94 or 3.99 m. **Weight:** 106.1–107.3 t.
Train Supply: Not equipped.
Notes: 37610–679/682–698/800–899 have roof mounted horns and are 3.99 m. high. Others have nose mounted horns and are 3.94 m. high.

37503	§	E	E	WKFN	TO	
37505		T	E	WKFN	IM	British Steel Workington

37509		F	E	WKFN	IM	
37510		IS	E	WKFN	ML	
37513	s	LH	E	WKFN	IM	
37515	s	FM	E	WKFN	IM	
37516	s	LH	E	WKFN	CF	
37517	s	LH	E	WKFN	IM	
37518		FM	E	WKFN	IM	
37519	§	FM	E	WKFN	TO	
37520		E	E	WKFN	ML	
37521		E	E	WKFN	CF	English China Clays

Class 37/6. Refurbished locos for the aborted Nightstar services. Main generator replaced by alternator, re-geared bogies and UIC jumpers. Details as class 37/5 except:
Max. Speed: 80 († 75) mph.   **Train Brake:** Air.
Train Supply: Not equipped, but electric through wired.
Multiple Working: TDM († plus DRS System).

37601		EU	EU	GPSV	OC
37602		EU	EU	GPSV	OC
37603		EU	EU	GPSV	OC
37604		EU	EU	DFLT	ML
37605		EU	EU	GPSV	OC
37606		EU	EU	GPSV	OC
37607	†	DR	DR	XHSD	SD
37608	†	DR	DR	XHSD	SD
37609	†	DR	DR	XHSD	SD
37610	†	DR	DR	XHSD	SD
37611	†	DR	DR	XHSD	SD
37612	†	DR	DR	XHSD	SD

Class 37/5 (Continued).

37667	s	E	E	WKFN	ML	Meldon Quarry Centenary
37668	s	E	E	WKFN	CF	
37669		E	E	WKFN	CF	
37670		E	E	WKFN	CF	St.Blazey T&RS Depot
37671		T	E	WKFN	CF	Tre Pol and Pen
37672	s	T	E	WKFN	CF	
37673		T	E	WKFN	CF	
37674		T	E	WKFN	CF	St. Blaise Church 1445-1995
37675	s	T	E	WKFN	IM	
37676		F	E	WKFN	IM	
37677	§	F	E	WKFN	TO	
37678		F	E	WKFN	IM	
37679		F	E	WKFN	IM	
37680	§	FA	E	WKFN	TO	
37682		E	E	WKFN	IM	Hartlepool Pipe Mill
37683		T	E	WKFN	IM	
37684		E	E	WKFN	ML	Peak National Park
37685		IS	E	WKFN	IM	
37686		FA	E	WKFN	IM	
37688	§	E	E	WKFN	IM	

37689		F	E	WKFN	IM	
37692	s	FC	E	WKFN	ML	The Lass O' Ballochmyle
37693	s	T	E	WKFN	ML	
37694		E	E	WKFN	IM	
37695	s	E	E	WKFN	IM	
37696	s	T	E	WKFN	CF	
37697	s§	E	E	WKFN	IM	
37698	s	LH	E	WKFN	IM	

Class 37/7. Refurbished locos. Main generator replaced by alternator. Re-geared (CP7) bogies. Ballast weights added. Details as class 37/5 except:
Main Alternator: GEC G564AZ (37796–803) Brush BA1005A (others).
Max. Tractive Effort: 276 kN (62000 lbf).
Weight: 120 t.   **RA:** 7.

37701	as	T	E	WKGN	CF	
37702	s	T	E	WKGN	ML	Taff Merthyr
37703		E	E	WKGN	EH	
37704	s	E	E	WKGN	CF	
37705		MG	E	WKGN	EH	
37706		E	E	WKGN	TO	
37707		E	E	WKGN	IM	
37708		FP	E	WKGN	IM	
37709		MG	E	WKGN	EH	
37710		LH	E	WKGN	IM	
37711		FM	E	WKGN	EH	
37712	a	E	E	WKGN	ML	
37713		LH	E	WKGN	IM	
37714	a	E	E	WKGN	ML	
37715		MG	E	WKGN	TO	British Petroleum
37716		E	E	WKGN	IM	
37717		E	E	WKGN	IM	Berwick Middle School, Railsafe Trophy Winners 1998
37718		E	E	WKGN	IM	
37719	a	FP	E	WKGN	IM	
37796	s	E	E	WKGN	ML	
37797	as	E	E	WKGN	ML	
37798		ML	E	WKGN	TO	
37799	s	T	E	WKGN	ML	Sir Dyfed/County of Dyfed
37800		MG	E	WKGN	EH	
37801	s	E	E	WKGN	ML	
37802	s	T	E	WKGN	ML	
37803		ML	E	WKGN	EH	
37883		E	E	WKGN	IM	
37884		LH	E	WKGN	IM	Gartcosh
37885		E	E	WKGN	IM	
37886		E	E	WKGN	IM	
37887	s	T	E	WKGN	CF	
37888		F	E	WKGN	CF	
37889		T	E	WKGN	CF	
37890	a	MG	E	WKGN	EH	The Railway Observer
37891		MG	E	WKGN	EH	

37892	**MG**	E	WKGN	EH	Ripple Lane[1]
37893	**E**	E	WKGN	ML	
37894	s **FC**	E	WKGN	CF	
37895	as **E**	E	WKGN	CF	
37896	s **T**	E	WKGN	CF	
37897	s **T**	E	WKGN	CF	
37898	s **T**	E	WKGN	TO	Cwmbargoed DP
37899	s **E**	E	WKGN	TO	

Class 37/9. Refurbished locos. New power unit. Main generator replaced by alternator. Ballast weights added. Details as Class 37/4 except:
Engine: Mirrlees MB275T of 1340 kW (1800 hp) at 1000 rpm (‡ Ruston RK270T of 1340 kW (1800 hp) at 900 rpm).
Main Alternator: Brush BA1005A (‡ GEC G564AZ).
Max. Tractive Effort: 279 kN (62680 lbf).
Cont. Tractive Effort: 184 kN (41250 lbf) at 11.4 mph.
Weight: 120 t.   **RA:** 7.
Train supply: Not equipped.

37901	**T**	E	WNXX	CF(S)	Mirrlees Pioneer
37902	**FM**	E	WKHN	CF	
37903	**FM**	E	WKHN	CF	
37904	**FM**	E	WNYX	CF(S)	
37905	‡s **FM**	E	WKHN	CF	
37906	‡s **T**	E	WKHN	CF	

CLASS 43   BREL/PAXMAN   Bo–Bo

Built: 1976–82 by BREL at Crewe Works.
Engine: Paxman Valenta 12RP200L of 1680 kW (2250 hp) at 1500 rpm († Paxman 12VP185 of 2010 kW (2700 hp) at ?? rpm).
Main Alternator: Brush BA1001B.
Traction Motors: Brush TMH68–46 or GEC G417AZ, frame mounted.
Max. Tractive Effort: 80 kN (17980 lbf).
Cont. Tractive Effort: 46 kN (10340 lbf) at 64.5 mph.
Power At Rail: 1320 kW (1770 hp).   **Train Brakes:** Air.
Brake Force: 35 t.   **Dimensions:** 17.79 x 2.71 x 3.88 m.
Weight: 70 t.   **Wheel Diameter:** 1020 mm.
Design Speed: 125 mph.   **Max. Speed:** 125 mph.
Fuel Capacity: 4500 litres.   **RA:** 5.
Train Supply: Three-phase electric.
Multiple Working: Within Class, jumpers at non-driving end only.

43002	**GW**	A	IWRP	PM	Techni?uest
43003	**GW**	A	IWRP	PM	
43004	**GW**	A	IWRP	PM	Borough of Swindon
43005	**GW**	A	IWRP	PM	
43006	**IS**	A	IWCP	LA	
43007	**IS**	A	IWCP	LA	
43008	**V**	A	IWCP	LA	
43009	**GW**	A	IWRP	PM	
43010	**GW**	A	IWRP	PM	

43011	**GW**	A	IWRP	PM	Reader 125
43012	**GW**	A	IWRP	PM	
43013	**V**	P	ICCP	LA	
43014	**IS**	P	ICCP	LA	
43015	**GW**	A	IWRP	PM	
43016	**GW**	A	IWRP	PM	
43017	**GW**	A	IWRP	LA	
43018	**GW**	A	IWRP	LA	The Red Cross
43019	**GW**	A	IWRP	LA	Dinas Abertawe/City of Swansea
43020	**GW**	A	IWRP	LA	John Grooms
43021	**GW**	A	IWRP	LA	
43022	**GW**	A	IWRP	LA	
43023	**GW**	A	IWRP	LA	County of Cornwall
43024	**GW**	A	IWRP	LA	
43025	**GW**	A	IWRP	LA	Exeter
43026	**GW**	A	IWRP	LA	City of Westminster
43027	**GW**	A	IWRP	LA	Glorious Devon
43028	**GW**	A	IWRP	LA	
43029	**IS**	A	IWRP	LA	
43030	**GW**	A	IWRP	PM	
43031	**GW**	A	IWRP	PM	
43032	**GW**	A	IWRP	PM	The Royal Regiment of Wales
43033	**IS**	A	IWRP	PM	
43034	**GW**	A	IWRP	PM	The Black Horse
43035	**IS**	A	IWRP	PM	
43036	**IS**	A	IWRP	PM	
43037	**IS**	A	IWRP	PM	
43038	**GN**	A	IECP	EC	
43039	**GN**	A	IECP	EC	
43040	**GW**	A	IWRP	PM	
43041	**IS**	A	IWRP	LA	City of Discovery
43042	**GW**	A	IWRP	LA	
43043	**MM**	P	IMLP	NL	LEICESTERSHIRE COUNTY CRICKET CLUB
43044	**MM**	P	IMLP	NL	Borough of Kettering
43045	**MM**	P	IMLP	NL	
43046	**MM**	P	IMLP	NL	Royal Philharmonic
43047 †	**MM**	P	IMLP	NL	
43048	**MM**	P	IMLP	NL	
43049	**MM**	P	IMLP	NL	Neville Hill
43050	**MM**	P	IMLP	NL	
43051	**MM**	P	IMLP	NL	
43052	**MM**	P	IMLP	NL	
43053	**MM**	P	IMLP	NL	Leeds United
43054	**MM**	P	IMLP	NL	
43055	**MM**	P	IMLP	NL	Sheffield Star
43056	**MM**	P	IMLP	NL	
43057	**MM**	P	IMLP	NL	
43058	**MM**	P	IMLP	NL	MIDLAND PRIDE
43059 †	**MM**	P	IMLP	NL	
43060	**MM**	P	IMLP	NL	County of Leicestershire

3061	**MM**	P	IMLP	NL	
3062	**V**	P	ICCP	LA	
3063	**V**	P	ICCP	LA	Maiden Voyager
3064	**MM**	P	IMLP	NL	
3065	**IS**	P	ICCP	LA	City of Edinburgh
3066	**MM**	P	IMLP	NL	Nottingham Playhouse
3067	**IS**	P	ICCP	LA	
3068	**V**	P	ICCP	LA	The Red Nose
3069	**V**	P	ICCP	LA	
3070	**IS**	P	ICCP	LA	
3071	**IS**	P	ICCP	LA	Forward Birmingham
3072	**MM**	P	IMLP	NL	Derby Etches Park
3073	**MM**	P	IMLP	NL	
3074 †	**MM**	P	IMLP	NL	BBC EAST MIDLANDS TODAY
3075 †	**MM**	P	IMLP	NL	
3076	**MM**	P	IMLP	NL	THE MASTER CUTLER 1947-1997
3077	**MM**	P	IMLP	NL	
3078	**IS**	P	ICCP	LA	Golowan Festival Penzance
3079	**IS**	P	ICCP	LA	
3080	**IS**	P	ICCP	LA	
3081	**MM**	P	IMLP	NL	
3082	**MM**	P	IMLP	NL	DERBYSHIRE FIRST
3083	**MM**	P	IMLP	NL	
3084	**V**	P	ICCP	LA	County of Derbyshire
3085	**MM**	P	IMLP	NL	
3086	**IS**	P	ICCP	LA	
3087	**IS**	P	ICCP	LA	
3088	**IS**	P	ICCP	LA	XIII Commonwealth Games Scotland 1986
3089	**IS**	P	ICCP	LA	
3090	**V**	P	ICCP	LA	
3091	**IS**	P	ICCP	LA	Edinburgh Military Tattoo
3092	**V**	P	ICCP	LA	Institution of Mechanical Engineers 150th Anniversary 1847-1997
3093	**V**	P	ICCP	LA	Lady in Red
3094	**IS**	P	ICCP	LA	
3095	**GN**	A	IECP	EC	
3096	**GN**	A	IECP	EC	The Great Racer
3097	**IS**	P	ICCP	LA	
3098	**V**	P	ICCP	LA	railway children
3099	**IS**	P	ICCP	LA	
3100	**V**	P	ICCP	LA	Blackpool Rock
3101	**V**	P	ICCP	LA	The Irish Mail Trên Post Gwyddelig
3102	**V**	P	ICCP	LA	
3103	**V**	P	ICCP	LA	
3104	**IS**	A	SCXL	LA(S)	County of Cleveland
3105	**GN**	A	IECP	EC	
3106	**GN**	A	IECP	EC	
3107	**GN**	A	IECP	EC	

43108	**GN**	A	IECP	EC	
43109	**GN**	A	IECP	EC	
43110	**GN**	A	IECP	EC	
43111	**GN**	A	IECP	EC	
43112	**GN**	A	IECP	EC	
43113	**GN**	A	IECP	EC	
43114	**GN**	A	IECP	EC	
43115	**GN**	A	IECP	EC	
43116	**GN**	A	IECP	EC	
43117	**GN**	A	IECP	EC	
43118	**GN**	A	IECP	EC	
43119	**GN**	A	IECP	EC	
43120	**GN**	A	IECP	EC	
43121	**IS**	P	ICCP	LA	West Yorkshire Metropolitan County
43122	**IS**	P	ICCP	LA	South Yorkshire Metropolitan County
43123	**IS**	P	ICCP	LA	
43124	**GW**	A	IWRP	PM	
43125	**IS**	A	IWRP	PM	Merchant Venturer
43126	**GW**	A	IWRP	PM	City of Bristol
43127	**IS**	A	IWRP	PM	
43128	**GW**	A	IWRP	PM	
43129	**GW**	A	IWRP	PM	
43130	**IS**	A	IWRP	PM	Sulis Minerva
43131	**GW**	A	IWRP	PM	Sir Felix Pole
43132	**GW**	A	IWRP	PM	
43133	**GW**	A	IWRP	PM	
43134	**GW**	A	IWRP	PM	County of Somerset
43135	**GW**	A	IWRP	PM	
43136	**GW**	A	IWRP	PM	
43137	**GW**	A	IWRP	PM	Newton Abbot 150
43138	**GW**	A	IWRP	PM	
43139	**GW**	A	IWRP	PM	
43140	**GW**	A	IWRP	PM	
43141	**GW**	A	IWRP	PM	
43142	**GW**	A	IWRP	PM	
43143	**IS**	A	IWRP	PM	
43144	**IS**	A	IWRP	PM	
43145	**GW**	A	IWRP	PM	
43146	**IS**	A	IWRP	PM	
43147	**IS**	A	IWRP	PM	
43148	**GW**	A	IWRP	PM	
43149	**GW**	A	IWRP	PM	B.B.C. Wales Today
43150	**GW**	A	IWRP	PM	Bristol Evening Post
43151	**GW**	A	IWRP	PM	
43152	**GW**	A	IWRP	PM	
43153	**V**	P	ICCP	LA	THE ENGLISH RIVIERA TORQUAY PAIGNTON BRIXHAM
43154	**V**	P	ICCP	LA	INTERCITY
43155	**V**	P	ICCP	LA	City of Aberdeen

43156	**IS**	P	ICCP	LA	
43157	**V**	P	ICCP	LA	HMS Penzance
43158	**V**	P	ICCP	LA	
43159	**IS**	P	ICCP	LA	
43160	**V**	P	ICCP	LA	
43161	**IS**	P	ICCP	LA	Reading Evening Post
43162	**IS**	P	ICCP	LA	Borough of Stevenage
43163	**IS**	A	IWRP	LA	
43164	**IS**	A	IWRP	LA	
43165	**IS**	A	IWRP	LA	
43166	**IS**	A	IWRP	LA	
43167 †	**GN**	A	IECP	EC	
43168 †	**GW**	A	IWRP	LA	
43169 †	**GW**	A	IWRP	LA	The National Trust
43170 †	**GW**	A	IWRP	LA	Edward Paxman
43171	**GW**	A	IWRP	LA	
43172	**IS**	A	IWRP	LA	
43173 †	**GW**	A	IWRP	ZC(S)	
43174	**GW**	A	IWRP	LA	Bristol-Bordeaux
43175 †	**IS**	A	IWRP	LA	
43176	**IS**	A	IWRP	LA	
43177 †	**GW**	A	IWRP	LA	University of Exeter
43178	**V**	A	IWCP	LA	
43179 †	**GW**	A	IWRP	LA	Pride of Laira
43180	**V**	P	ICCP	LA	City of Newcastle upon Tyne
43181	**IS**	A	IWRP	LA	Devonport Royal Dockyard 1693-1993
43182	**IS**	A	IWRP	LA	
43183	**GW**	A	IWRP	LA	
43184	**V**	A	IWCP	LA	
43185	**GW**	A	IWRP	LA	Great Western
43186	**GW**	A	IWRP	LA	Sir Francis Drake
43187	**GW**	A	IWRP	LA	
43188	**GW**	A	IWRP	LA	City of Plymouth
43189	**GW**	A	IWRP	LA	RAILWAY HERITAGE TRUST
43190	**GW**	A	IWRP	LA	
43191 †	**GW**	A	IWRP	LA	Seahawk
43192	**GW**	A	IWRP	LA	City of Truro
43193	**IS**	P	ICCP	LA	Plymouth SPIRIT OF DISCOVERY
43194	**IS**	P	ICCP	LA	
43195	**IS**	P	ICCP	LA	British Red Cross 125th Birthday 1995
43196	**IS**	P	ICCP	LA	The Newspaper Society Founded 1836
43197	**IS**	P	ICCP	LA	Railway Magazine Centenary 1897-1997
43198	**IS**	P	ICCP	LA	

CLASS 46   BR/SULZER   1Co–Co

Built: 1963 by BR at Derby Locomotive Works.
Engine: Sulzer 12LDA28B of 1860 kW (2500 hp) at 750 rpm.
Main Generator: Brush TG160-60.
Traction Motors: Brush TM73-68 Mk3 (axle hung).
Max. Tractive Effort: 245 kN (55000 lbf).
Cont. Tractive Effort: 141 kN (31600 lbf) at 22.3 mph.
Power At Rail: 1460 kW (1960 hp).   **Train Brakes:** Air & vacuum.
Brake Force: 63 t.   **Dimensions:** 20.70 x 2.78 x 3.92 m.
Weight: 140 t.   **Wheel Diameter:** 914/1143 mm.
Design Speed: 90 mph.   **Max. Speed:** 75 mph.
Fuel Capacity: 3591 litres.   **RA:** 7.
Train Supply: Not equipped.   **Multiple Working:** Not equipped.
Non-standard livery/numbering:
•   46035 carries number D172. Official RSL number is 89472.

46035	**G**	RS	MBDL	CN		Ixion

CLASS 47   BR/BRUSH/SULZER   Co–C

Built: 1963–67 by Brush Traction, at Loughborough or by BR at Crewe Work
Engine: Sulzer 12LDA28C of 1920 kW (2580 hp) at 750 rpm.
Main Generator: Brush TG160-60 Mk4 or TM172-50 Mk1.
Traction Motors: Brush TM64-68 Mk1 or Mk1A.
Max. Tractive Effort: 267 kN (60000 lbf).
Cont. Tractive Effort: 133 kN (30000 lbf) at 26 mph.
Power At Rail: 1550 kW (2080 hp).   **Train Brakes:** Air.
Brake Force: 61 t.   **Dimensions:** 19.38 x 2.79 x 3.9 m.
Weight: 111.5–120.6 t.   **Wheel Diameter:** 1143 mm.
Design Speed: 95 mph.   **Max. Speed:** 75 mph.
Fuel Capacity: 3273 (+ 5550, † 4410 litres).**RA:** 6.
Train Supply: Not equipped.
Multiple Working: Green Circle (n not equipped).
Non-standard liveries/numbering:
•   47016 also carries number 1546.
•   47114 is two-tone green with Freightliner logos.
•   47145 is dark blue with Railfreight Distribution logos.
•   47484 is Great Western Railway style green, with cast numberplates.
•   47803 is yellow and white with a red stripe.
•   47972 is in British Railways Board Central Services livery of red and gre

**Class 47/0 (Dual braked locos) or Class 47/2 (Air braked locos). Standar
Design. Details as above.**

47004	x **G**	E	WHBF	BS	Old Oak Common Traction & Rolling Stock Depot
47016	x **FO**	E	WHBF	BS	ATLAS[1]
47033	m+ **FE**	E	WHBF	BS	The Royal Logistic Corps
47049	m+ **FE**	E	WNXX	BA(S)	GEFCO
47051	m+ **FE**	E	WHBF	BS	

47052		FF	P	DFLT	CD	
47053	m+	FE	E	WNYX	BS(S)	Dollands Moor International
47060		FF	P	DHLT	EH(S)	
47079	x	FF	FL	DFFT	CD	
47085	m+	FE	E	WNXX	BA(S)	REPTA 1893-1993
47095	m+	FE	E	WNYX	BS(S)	
47114	m+	0	FL	DFLM	CD	Freightlinerbulk
47125	m+	FE	E	WNXX	BA(S)	
47145	m+	0	E	WHBF	BS	Merddin Emrys
47146	m+	FE	E	WNYX	CD(S)	Loughborough Grammar School
47150	m+	FE	FL	DFLM	CD	
47152	m+	FF	FL	DFLM	CD	
47156	m+	FD	FL	DFYX	BA(S)	
47157	m+	FF	FL	DFLM	CD	Johnson Stevens Agencies
47186	m+	FE	E	WNYX	BS(S)	Catcliffe Demon
47188	m+	FE	E	WNYX	CD(S)	
47193	x	F	FL	DFLT	CD	
47194	m+	FD	E	WHBF	BS	
47197	x	FF	P	DFFT	CD	
47200	m+	FE	E	WHBF	BS	Herbert Austin
47201	m+	FE	E	WNYX	BS(S)	
47204	m+	FF	FL	DFLM	CD	
47205	m+	FF	FL	DFLM	CD	
47206		FF	P	DFLT	CD	The Morris Dancer
47207	m+	FF	FL	DFLM	CD	The Felixstowe Partnership
47209	m+	FF	P	DFLM	CD	
47210	m+	FD	E	WHBF	BS	
47211	m+	FD	E	WNYX	EH(S)	
47212	x†	FF	P	DFLT	CD	
47213	m+	FD	E	WHBF	BS	Marchwood Military Port
47217	m+	FE	E	WHBF	BS	
47218	m+	FE	E	WHBF	BS	United Transport Europe
47219	m+	FE	E	WHBF	BS	Arnold Kunzler
47221	x†	FP	FL	DHLT	TO(S)	
47223	x†	F	E	WNYX	BA(S)	
47224	x†	FP	FL	DFLT	EH(S)	
47225		FF	P	DHLT	CD	
47226	m+	FD	E	WHBF	BS	
47228	m+	FE	E	WHBF	BS	axial
47229	m+	FD	E	WNYX	BS(S)	
47231		FF	P	DFLT	CD	
47234	m+	FF	FL	DFLM	CD	
47236	m+	FE	E	WHBF	BS	ROVER GROUP QUALITY ASSURED
47237	m+	FE	E	WHBF	BS	
47238	x	FD	E	WNYX	BS(S)	
47241	m+	FE	E	WNYX	BS(S)	Halewood Silver Jubilee 1988
47245	m+	FE	E	WHBF	BS	The Institute of Export
47256	x	FD	E	WNZX	DR(S)	
47258	m+	FE	FL	DFLM	CD	
47270		FF	P	DFFT	CD	Cory Brothers 1842-1992
47276	m†	F	E	WHBF	BS	

47277	x†	**FD**	E	WNYX	IM(S)	
47278	x	**FP**	E	WNYX	SP(S)	
47279	m+	**FF**	FL	DFLM	CD	
47280	m+	**FD**	E	WHBF	BS	Pedigree
47281	m+	**FD**	E	WHBF	BS	
47283		**FF**	P	DFLT	CD	
47284	m+	**FD**	E	WHBF	BS	
47285	m+	**FE**	E	WHBF	BS	
47286	m+	**FE**	E	WHBF	BS	Port of Liverpool
47287	m+	**FE**	FL	DFLM	CD	
47289	m+	**FF**	P	DFLM	CD	
47290	m+	**FF**	FL	DFLM	CD	
47292	m+	**F**	FL	DFLM	CD	
47293	m+	**FE**	E	WHBF	BS	TRANSFESA
47294	s†	**FD**	E	WNYX	TT(S)	
47295	x†	**F**	FL	DFFT	CD	
47296	x	**FF**	P	DFLT	CD	
47297	m+	**FE**	E	WHBF	BS	Cobra RAILFREIGHT
47298	m+	**FD**	E	WHBF	BS	Pegasus
47299	m†	**FE**	E	WNXX	LB(S)	

Class 47/3 (Dual braked locos) or Class 47/2 (Air braked locos). Details as Class 47/0 except: **Weight:** 113.7 t.

47300	x	**CE**	E	WNYX	BS(S)	
47301	m+	**FF**	P	DFLM	CD	Freightliner Birmingham
47302	m+	**FF**	FL	DFLM	CD	
47303	m+	**FF**	FL	DFLM	CD	Freightliner Cleveland
47304	m+	**FD**	E	WHBF	BS	
47305		**FF**	P	DFLT	CD	
47306	m+	**FE**	E	WHBF	BS	The Sapper
47307	m+	**FE**	E	WHBF	BS	
47308	m+	**FF**	FL	DFLT	CD	
47309	m+	**FD**	FL	DHLT	CD	European Freight Operator of the Year - IFW Freighting Industry Awards 1998
47310	m+	**FE**	E	WHBF	BS	Henry Ford
47312	m+	**FE**	E	WHBF	BS	Parsec of Europe
47313	m+	**FD**	E	WHBF	BS	
47314	m+	**FD**	E	WHBF	BS	Transmark
47315	xs	**CE**	E	WHMN	IM	
47316	m+	**FE**	E	WHBF	BS	
47318	x	**FO**	E	WNZX	BS(S)	
47319	x†	**FP**	E	WNZX	IM(S)	Norsk Hydro
47323	m+	**FF**	FL	DFFT	CD	
47326	m+	**FE**	E	WHBF	BS	Saltley Depot Quality Approved
47328	m+	**FD**	E	WNXX	CD(S)	
47329	x	**CE**	FL	DFLT	CD	
47330	m+	**FF**	FL	DFLM	CD	
47331	xs	**CE**	E	WHMN	IM	
47332	x	**CE**	FL	DFLT	CD	
47334		**FF**	FL	DFLT	CD	P & O Nedlloyd

47335	m+ **FD**	E	WHBF	BS	
47337	m+ **FF**	FL	DFLM	CD	
47338	m+ **FE**	E	WHBF	BS	
47339	m+ **FF**	P	DFLT	CD	
47341	x	**CE**	E	WNYX	TT(S)	
47344	m+ **FE**	E	WHBF	BS	
47345	x	**FF**	P	DFLT	CD	
47348	m+ **FE**	E	WHBF	BS	St. Christopher's Railway Home
47349	x	**FF**	P	DFLT	CD	
47351	m+ **FE**	E	WNYX	LB(S)	
47352	x	**CE**	E	WNZX	FH(S)	
47353	x	**FF**	FL	DFLT	CD	
47354		**FF**	FL	DFLT	CD	
47355	m+ **FD**	E	WHBF	BS	
47357	x	**CE**	E	WNYX	BS(S)	
47358	m+ **FF**	P	DFLM	CD	
47360	m+ **FE**	E	WHBF	BS	
47361	m+ **FF**	FL	DFLM	CD	Wilton Endeavour
47362	m+ **FD**	E	WHBF	BS	
47363	m+ **F**	E	WHBF	BS	
47365	m+ **FE**	E	WNYX	CF(S)	Diamond Jubilee
47366	x	**CE**	E	WNYX	SP(S)	
47367	m+ **FF**	FL	DFLM	CD	
47368	x	**F**	E	WNYX	SF(S)	
47370	m+ **FF**	FL	DFLM	CD	Andrew A Hodgkinson
47371	x	**FF**	P	DFLT	CD	
47372	x	**FF**	FL	DFLT	CD	
47375	m+ **FE**	E	WHBF	BS	Tinsley Traction Depot (Quality Approved)
47376	x	**FF**	P	DFLT	CD	Freightliner 1995
47377		**FF**	P	DFLT	CD	
47379	m† **F**	E	WHBF	BS	

Class 47/4. Electric Train Supply equipment. Details as Class 47/0 except:
Weight: 120.4–125.1 t.   **Max. Speed:** 95 (* 75, † 100) mph.
Fuel Capacity: 3273 (+ 5887) litres.   **RA:** 7.
Train Supply: Electric, index 66.
Multiple Working: Not equipped († Blue Star).

47462	x* **RG**	E	WNYX	TT(S)	
47467	x* **BL**	E	WHMN	IM	
47471	x	**I**	E	WNYX	BA(S)	
47474	x* **RG**	E	WHMN	IM	Sir Rowland Hill
47475	x* **RX**	E	WHMN	IM	Restive
47476	x* **RG**	E	WHMN	IM	Night Mail
47478	x* **B**	E	WNYX	BS(S)	
47481	x	**BL**	E	WNYX	BA(S)	
47484	x* **0**	E	WNXX	CD(S)	ISAMBARD KINGDOM BRUNEL
47488	x	**G**	FG	SDFR	TM	
47489		**RG**	E	WNYX	BS(S)	
47492	x* **RX**	E	WHMN	IM	
47501	x	**RG**	E	WHCN	CD	

47513	x*	**BL**	E	WNYX	CD(S)
47515	x	**IM**	E	WNYX	BA(S)
47519	x+*	**G**	E	WHBF	BS
47522	x*	**RG**	E	WHMN	IM	Doncaster Enterprise
47523	*	**IM**	E	WHBF	BS
47524	x*	**RX**	E	WNYX	BA(S)
47525	x*	**FE**	E	WNYX	CD(S)
47526	x*	**BL**	E	WNYX	BA(S)
47528	x*	**IM**	E	WNYX	DR(S)	The Queen's Own Mercian Yeomanry
47530	x*	**RX**	E	WNYX	BA(S)
47532	x*	**RX**	E	WNYX	CD(S)
47535	x*	**RX**	E	WHMN	IM
47536	x*	**RX**	E	WNYX	CD(S)
47539		**RX**	E	WNYX	BA(S)
47540	xm*	**CE**	E	WNYX	BA(S)	The Institution of Civil Engineers
47547		**N**	E	WNZX	CD(S)
47550	x*	**IM**	E	WNYX	IM(S)
47555	x*	**FE**	E	WHMN	IM	The Commonwealth Spirit
47565	x	**RX**	E	WHDT	CD	Responsive
47566	x*	**RX**	E	WNYX	CD(S)
47572	x	**RG**	E	WHCN	CD	Ely Cathedral
47574	x*	**RG**	E	WNXX	CD(S)
47575	x	**RG**	E	WHCN	CD	City of Hereford
47576	x*	**RX**	E	WNYX	CD(S)
47584	x	**RX**	E	WHCN	CD	THE LOCOMOTIVE & CARRIAGE INSTITUTION
47596	x	**RX**	E	WHCN	CD
47624	xj*	**RX**	E	WNYX	AN(S)	Saint Andrew
47627	x	**R**	E	WHCN	CD
47628	j*	**RX**	E	WNYX	BA(S)
47634	x	**RG**	E	WHCN	CD	Holbeck
47635	xj	**RG**	E	WHCN	CD
47640	j*	**RG**	E	WHBF	BS	University of Strathclyde

Class 47/7. Electric Train Supply and Push & Pull equipment (RCH System). Details as Class 47/4 except:
Weight: 118.7 t.   **Fuel Capacity:** 5887 litres.

47701	x	**FG**	FG	SDFR	TM	Waverley
47702	x	**V**	E	ILRA	TO	County of Suffolk
47703	x	**FG**	FG	SDFR	TM
47704	*	**RX**	E	WNZX	CD(S)
47707	x	**RX**	E	WNYX	BA(S)	Holyrood
47709	x	**FG**	FG	SDFR	TM
47710	x	**FG**	FG	SDFR	TM
47711	x	**V**	E	ILRA	TO	County of Hertfordshire
47712	x	**FG**	FG	SDFR	TM
47714	x	**RX**	E	WNYX	BA(S)
47715	*	**N**	E	WNYX	BA(S)
47716	x*	**RX**	E	WNYX	BA(S)
47717	x	**RG**	E	WNYX	BA(S)

Class 47/7. Electric Train Supply equipment and RCH Jumper Cables for use on Railnet services. Details as Class 47/4 except:
Weight: 118.7 t.   **Fuel Capacity:** 5887 litres.

47721		**RX**	E	WHDP	CD	Saint Bede
47722		**RX**	E	WHDP	CD	The Queen Mother
47725		**RX**	E	WHDP	CD	The Railway Mission
47726		**RX**	E	WHDP	CD	Manchester Airport Progress
47727		**RX**	E	WHDP	CD	Duke of Edinburgh's Award
47732	x	**RX**	E	WHDP	CD	Restormel
47733		**RX**	E	WHDP	CD	Eastern Star
47734		**RX**	E	WHDP	CD	Crewe Diesel Depot Quality Approved
47736		**RX**	E	WHDP	CD	Cambridge Traction & Rolling Stock Depot
47737		**RX**	E	WHDP	CD	Resurgent
47738		**RX**	E	WHDP	CD	Bristol Barton Hill
47739		**RX**	E	WHDP	CD	Resourceful
47741		**RX**	E	WHDP	CD	Resilient
47742		**RX**	E	WHDP	CD	The Enterprising Scot
47744		**E**	E	WHDP	CD	
47745	x	**RX**	E	WHDP	CD	Royal London Society for the Blind
47746		**RX**	E	WHDP	CD	The Bobby
47747		**RX**	E	WHDP	CD	Res Publica
47749		**RX**	E	WHDP	CD	Atlantic College
47750		**RX**	E	WHDP	CD	Royal Mail Cheltenham
47756		**RX**	E	WHDC	ML	Royal Mail Tyneside
47757		**RX**	E	WHDP	CD	Restitution
47758		**E**	E	WHDP	CD	Regency Rail Cruises
47759		**RX**	E	WHDP	CD	
47760		**RX**	E	WHDP	CD	Restless
47761		**RX**	E	WHDP	CD	
47762	x	**RX**	E	WHDP	CD	
47763		**RX**	E	WHDP	CD	
47764		**RX**	E	WHDP	CD	Resounding
47765	x	**RX**	E	WHDP	CD	Ressaldar
47766	x	**RX**	E	WHDP	CD	Resolute
47767		**RX**	E	WHDC	ML	Saint Columba
47768	x	**E**	E	WHDP	CD	Resonant
47769		**RX**	E	WHDP	CD	Resolve
47770		**RX**	E	WHDP	CD	Reserved
47771		**RX**	E	WHDP	CD	Heaton Traincare Depot
47772	x	**RX**	E	WHDP	CD	
47773		**RX**	E	WHDP	CD	Reservist
47774	x	**RX**	E	WHDP	CD	Poste Restante
47775		**RX**	E	WHDP	CD	Respite
47776	x	**RX**	E	WHDP	CD	Respected
47777	x	**RX**	E	WHDP	CD	Restored
47778		**RX**	E	WHDP	CD	Irresistible
47779		**RX**	E	WHDP	CD	
47780		**RX**	E	WHDP	CD	
47781		**RX**	E	WHDP	CD	Isle of Iona

47782	**RX**	E	WHDP	CD	
47783	**RX**	E	WHDP	CD	Saint Peter
47784	**RX**	E	WHDP	CD	Condover Hall
47785	**E**	E	WHDP	CD	Fiona Castle
47786	**E**	E	WHDP	CD	Roy Castle OBE
47787	**RX**	E	WHDP	CD	Victim Support
47788	**RX**	E	WHDP	CD	Captain Peter Manisty RN
47789	**RX**	E	WHDP	CD	Lindisfarne
47790	**RX**	E	WHDC	ML	Dewi Sant/Saint David
47791	**RX**	E	WHDC	ML	
47792	**RX**	E	WHDP	CD	Saint Cuthbert
47793	**RX**	E	WHDP	CD	Saint Augustine

Class 47/7. Electric Train Supply equipment. Locos dedicated for Royal Train & (occasional) Charter Train use. Details as Class 47/4 except:
Weight: 118.7 t. **Fuel Capacity**: 5887 litres.

47798	**RP**	E	WHDA	CD	Prince William
47799	**RP**	E	WHDA	CD	Prince Henry

Class 47/4 ("47/8" & "47/9") Continued.
Note: 47977 is expected to be renumbered from 47565 during 1999.

47802	*	**IS**	E	WHMN	IM	
47803	*	**O**	E	WNYX	SF(S)	
47805		**IS**	P	ILRA	TO	
47806		**V**	P	ILRA	TO	
47807		**V**	P	ILRA	TO	The Lion of Vienna
47810		**IS**	P	ILRA	TO	PORTERBROOK
47811		**GW**	P	IWLA	LE	
47812		**IS**	P	ILRA	TO	
47813		**GW**	P	IWLA	LE	S.S. Great Britain
47814		**V**	P	ILRA	TO	Totnes Castle
47815		**GW**	P	IWLA	LE	
47816		**IS**	P	IWLA	LE	Bristol Bath Road Quality Approved
47817		**V**	P	ILRA	TO	
47818		**IS**	P	ILRA	TO	
47822		**V**	P	ILRA	TO	Pride of Shrewsbury
47825		**IS**	P	ILRB	TO	Thomas Telford
47826		**IS**	P	ILRA	TO	
47827		**V**	P	ILRA	TO	
47828		**IS**	P	ILRA	TO	
47829		**IS**	P	ILRA	TO	
47830		**GW**	P	IWLA	LE	
47831		**IS**	P	ILRA	TO	Bolton Wanderer
47832		**IS**	P	IWLX	LE	Tamar[1]
47839		**IS**	P	ILRA	TO	
47840		**IS**	P	ILRA	TO	NORTH STAR
47841		**IS**	P	ILRA	TO	The Institution of Mechanical Engineers
47843		**IS**	P	ILRA	TO	
47844		**V**	P	ILRA	TO	
47845		**V**	P	ILRA	TO	County of Kent
47846		**GW**	P	IWLA	LE	THOR

47847	**IS**	P	ILRA	TO	
47848	**IS**	P	ILRA	TO	
47849	**IS**	P	ILRA	TO	
47851	**IS**	P	ILRA	TO	
47853	**IS**	P	ILRA	TO	
47854	**IS**	P	ILRA	TO	Women's Royal Voluntary Service
47971	xt **BL**	E	WNYX	CD(S)	Robin Hood
47972	t **0**	E	WNYX	CD(S)	The Royal Army Ordnance Corps
47976	xt **CE**	E	WHDT	CD	Aviemore Centre
47977					

Class 47/3 ("47/9") Continued.

| 47981 | xs* **CE** | E | WNYX | LB(S) | |

CLASS 50   ENGLISH ELECTRIC   Co–Co

Built: 1967–68 by English Electric at Vulcan Foundry, Newton-le-Willows.
Engine: English Electric 16CVST of 2010 kW (2700 hp) at 850 rpm.
Main Generator: English Electric 840/4B.
Traction Motors: English Electric 538/5A.
Max. Tractive Effort: 216 kN (48500 lbf).
Cont. Tractive Effort: 147 kN (33000 lbf) at 23.5 mph.
Power At Rail: 1540 kW (2070 hp).   **Train Brakes:** Air & vacuum.
Brake Force: 59 t.   **Dimensions:** 20.88 x 2.78 x 3.96 m.
Weight: 116.9 t.   **Wheel Diameter:** 1092 mm.
Design Speed: 105 mph.   **Max. Speed:** 90 (* 75) mph.
Fuel Capacity: 4796 litres.   **RA:** 6.
Train Supply: Electric, index 66.   **Multiple Working:** Orange Square.

| 50031 | * **BL** | 50 | MBDL | KR | Hood |
| 50050 | **BL** | HC | MBDL | SF | Fearless |

CLASS 55   ENGLISH ELECTRIC   Co–Co

Built: 1961 by English Electric at Vulcan Foundry, Newton-le-Willows.
Engine: Two Napier-Deltic T18-25 of 1230 kW (1650 hp) at 1500 rpm.
Main Generators: Two English Electric EE829.
Traction Motors: English Electric E538/A.
Max. Tractive Effort: 222 kN (50000 lbf).
Cont. Tractive Effort: 136 kN (30500 lbf) at 32.5 mph.
Power At Rail: 1969 kW (2640 hp).   **Train Brakes:** Air & vacuum.
Brake Force: 51 t.   **Dimensions:** 21.18 x 2.68 x 3.94 m.
Weight: 105 t.   **Wheel Diameter:** 1092 mm.
Design Speed: 100 mph.   **Max. Speed:** 100 mph.
Fuel Capacity: 3755 litres.   **RA:** 5.
Train Supply: Electric, index 66.   **Multiple Working:** Not equipped.
Non-standard livery/numbering:
•   55022 carries number D9000. Official RSL number is 89500.

| 55022 | **G** | 90 | MBDL | SF | ROYAL SCOTS GREY |

CLASS 56   BRUSH/BR/PAXMAN   Co–Co

Built: 1976–84 by Electroputere at Craiova, Romania (as sub contractors for Brush) or BREL at Doncaster or Crewe Works.
Engine: Ruston Paxman 16RK3CT of 2460 kW (3250 hp) at 900 rpm.
Main Alternator: Brush BA1101A.
Traction Motors: Brush TM73-62.
Max. Tractive Effort: 275 kN (61800 lbf).
Cont. Tractive Effort: 240 kN (53950 lbf) at 16.8 mph.
Power At Rail: 1790 kW (2400 hp).   **Train Brakes:** Air.
Brake Force: 60 t.   **Dimensions:** 19.36 x 2.79 x 3.9 m.
Weight: 125.2 t.   **Wheel Diameter:** 1143 mm.
Design Speed: 80 mph.   **Max. Speed:** 80 mph.
Fuel Capacity: 5228 litres.   **RA:** 7.
Train Supply: Not equipped.   **Multiple Working:** Red Diamond.
Note: All equipped with Slow Speed Control.

56003	LH	E	WGAN	IM	
56004	B	E	WGAN	IM	
56006	LH	E	WGAN	IM	Ferrybridge "C" Power Station
56007	T	E	WGAN	IM	
56008	B	E	WNYX	IM(S)	
56010	T	E	WGAN	IM	
56011	E	E	WGAN	IM	
56012	FC	E	WNYX	IM(S)	
56013	FC	E	WNYX	TT(S)	
56014	FC	E	WNYX	IM(S)	
56018	E	E	WGAN	IM	
56019	FR	E	WGAN	IM	
56021	LH	E	WGAN	IM	
56022	T	E	WGAN	IM	
56023	FC	E	WNYX	TT(S)	
56025	T	E	WGAN	IM	
56027	LH	E	WGAN	IM	
56029	T	E	WGAN	IM	
56031	CE	E	WGAN	IM	
56032	E	E	WGAN	IM	
56033	T	E	WGAN	IM	Shotton Paper Mill
56034	LH	E	WGAN	IM	Castell Ogwr/Ogmore Castle
56035	LH	E	WGAN	IM	
56036	TC	E	WGAN	IM	
56037	E	E	WGAN	IM	
56038	E	E	WNXX	LB(S)	Western Mail
56039	LH	E	WGAN	IM	
56040	T	E	WGAN	IM	Oystermouth
56041	E	E	WGAN	IM	
56043	FM	E	WGAN	IM	
56044	T	E	WGAN	IM	Cardiff Canton Quality Approved
56045	LH	E	WGAN	IM	British Steel Shelton
56046	CE	E	WGAN	IM	

56047	TC	E	WGAN	IM	
56048	E	E	WGAN	IM	
56049	TC	E	WGAN	IM	
56050	LH	E	WGAN	IM	British Steel Teesside
56051	E	E	WGAN	IM	
56052	T	E	WGAN	IM	The Cardiff Rod Mill
56053	T	E	WGAN	IM	Sir Morgannwg Ganol/ County of Mid Glamorgan
56054	T	E	WGAN	IM	British Steel Llanwern
56055	LH	E	WGAN	IM	
56056	T	E	WGAN	IM	
56057	E	E	WGAN	IM	British Fuels
56058	E	E	WGAN	IM	
56059	E	E	WGAN	IM	
56060	E	E	WGAN	IM	
56061	FM	E	WGAN	IM	
56062	E	E	WGAN	IM	
56063	E	E	WGAN	IM	Bardon Hill
56064	T	E	WGAN	IM	
56065	E	E	WGAN	IM	
56066	T	E	WGAN	IM	
56067	E	E	WGAN	IM	
56068	E	E	WGAN	IM	
56069	E	E	WGAN	IM	Wolverhampton Steel Terminal
56070	T	E	WGAN	IM	
56071	E	E	WGAN	IM	
56072	T	E	WGAN	IM	
56073	T	E	WGAN	IM	Tremorfa Steel Works
56074	LH	E	WGAN	IM	Kellingley Colliery
56075	F	E	WGAN	IM	West Yorkshire Enterprise
56076	T	E	WGAN	IM	British Steel Trostre
56077	LH	E	WGAN	IM	Thorpe Marsh Power Station
56078	E	E	WGAN	IM	
56079	T	E	WGAN	IM	
56080	F	E	WGAN	IM	Selby Coalfield
56081	F	E	WGAN	IM	
56082	F	E	WGAN	IM	
56083	LH	E	WGAN	IM	
56084	LH	E	WGAN	IM	
56085	LH	E	WGAN	IM	
56086	T	E	WGAN	IM	The Magistrates' Association
56087	E	E	WGAN	IM	ABP Port of Hull
56088	E	E	WGAN	IM	
56089	E	E	WGAN	IM	
56090	LH	E	WGAN	IM	
56091	E	E	WGAN	IM	Stanton
56092	T	E	WGAN	IM	
56093	T	E	WGAN	IM	
56094	E	E	WGAN	IM	Eggborough Power Station
56095	E	E	WGAN	IM	
56096	E	E	WGAN	IM	

56097	FM	E	WGAN	IM	
56098	F	E	WGAN	IM	
56099	T	E	WGAN	IM	Fiddlers Ferry Power Station
56100	LH	E	WGAN	IM	
56101	T	E	WGAN	IM	Mutual Improvement
56102	LH	E	WGAN	IM	
56103	E	E	WGAN	IM	Stora
56104	FC	E	WGAN	IM	
56105	E	E	WGAN	IM	
56106	LH	E	WGAN	IM	
56107	LH	E	WGAN	IM	
56108	F	E	WGAN	IM	
56109	LH	E	WGAN	IM	
56110	LH	E	WNXX	ZC(S)	Croft
56111	LH	E	WGAN	IM	
56112	LH	E	WGAN	IM	Stainless Pioneer
56113	E	E	WGAN	IM	
56114	E	E	WGAN	IM	
56115	E	E	WGAN	IM	
56116	LH	E	WGAN	IM	
56117	E	E	WGAN	IM	
56118	LH	E	WGAN	IM	
56119	E	E	WGAN	IM	
56120	E	E	WGAN	IM	
56121	T	E	WGAN	IM	
56123	T	E	WGAN	IM	Drax Power Station
56124	T	E	WGAN	IM	
56125	T	E	WGAN	IM	
56126	FC	E	WGAN	IM	
56127	T	E	WGAN	IM	
56128	T	E	WGAN	IM	
56129	T	E	WGAN	IM	
56130	LH	E	WGAN	IM	Wardley Opencast
56131	F	E	WGAN	IM	Ellington Colliery
56132	T	E	WGAN	IM	
56133	T	E	WGAN	IM	Crewe Locomotive Works
56134	FC	E	WGAN	IM	Blyth Power
56135	F	E	WGAN	IM	Port of Tyne Authority

CLASS 57   BRUSH/GM   Co–Co

Built: 1965 by Brush Traction at Loughborough as Class 47. Rebuilt 1997–99 by Brush Traction at Loughborough.
Engine: General Motors 645-12E3 of 1860 kW (2500 hp) at 900 rpm.
Main Alternator: Brush BA1101A.
Traction Motors: Brush TM68-46.
Maximum Tractive Effort: 244.5 kN (55000 lbf).
Continuous Tractive Effort: 140 kN (31500 lbf) at ?? mph.
Power at Rail: 1507 kW (2025 hp).   **Train Brakes:** Air.
Brake Force: 80 t.   **Dimensions:** 19.38 x 2.79 x 3.9 m.

Weight: 120.6 t.
Design Speed: 75 mph.
Fuel Capacity:
Train Supply: Not equipped.
Wheel Diameter: 1143 mm.
Max. Speed: 75 mph.
RA: 6
Multiple Working: Not equipped.

57001	(47356)	**FL**	FL	DFHZ	CD	Freightliner Pioneer
57002	(47322)	**FL**	FL	DFHZ	CD	Freightliner Phoenix
57003	(47317)	**FL**	FL	DFHZ	LB(S)	
57004	(47347)	**FL**	FL	DFHZ	LB(S)	
57005	(47350)	**FL**	FL	DFHZ	LB(S)	
57006	(47187)	**FL**	FL	DFHZ	LB(S)	

CLASS 58   BREL/PAXMAN   Co–Co

Built: 1983–87 by BREL at Doncaster Works.
Engine: Ruston Paxman RK3ACT of 2460 kW (3300 hp) at 1000 rpm.
Main Alternator: Brush BA1101B.
Traction Motors: Brush TM73-62.
Max. Tractive Effort: 275 kN (61800 lbf).
Cont. Tractive Effort: 240 kN (53950 lbf) at 17.4 mpn.
Power At Rail: 1780 kW (2387 hp).   **Train Brakes:** Air.
Brake Force: 62 t.   **Dimensions:** 19.13 x 2.72 x 3.93 m.
Weight: 130 t.   **Wheel Diameter:** 1120 mm.
Design Speed: 80 mph.   **Max. Speed:** 80 mph.
Fuel Capacity: 4214 litres.   **RA:** 7.
Train Supply: Not equipped.   **Multiple Working:** Red Diamond.
Note: All equipped with Slow Speed Control.

58001	**MG**	E	WFAN	TO	
58002	**ML**	E	WFAN	TO	Daw Mill Colliery
58003	**MG**	E	WFAN	TO	Markham Colliery
58004	**MG**	E	WFAN	TO	
58005	**ML**	E	WFAN	TO	Ironbridge Power Station
58006	**MG**	E	WFAN	TO	
58007	**MG**	E	WFAN	TO	Drakelow Power Station
58008	**ML**	E	WFAN	TO	
58009	**MG**	E	WFAN	TO	
58010	**MG**	E	WFAN	TO	
58011	**MG**	E	WFAN	TO	Worksop Depot
58012	**MG**	E	WFAN	TO	
58013	**ML**	E	WFAN	TO	
58014	**ML**	E	WFAN	TO	Didcot Power Station
58015	**MG**	E	WFAN	TO	
58016	**E**	E	WFAN	TO	
58017	**MG**	E	WFAN	TO	Eastleigh Depot
58018	**MG**	E	WFAN	TO	High Marnham Power Station
58019	**MG**	E	WFAN	TO	Shirebrook Colliery
58020	**MG**	E	WFAN	TO	Doncaster Works
58021	**ML**	E	WFAN	TO	Hither Green Depot
58022	**MG**	E	WFAN	TO	
58023	**ML**	E	WFAN	TO	Peterborough Depot

58024	E	E	WFAN	TO	
58025	MG	E	WFAN	TO	
58026	MG	E	WFAN	TO	
58027	MG	E	WFAN	TO	
58028	MG	E	WFAN	TO	
58029	MG	E	WFAN	TO	
58030	E	E	WFAN	TO	
58031	MG	E	WFAN	TO	
58032	ML	E	WFAN	TO	Thoresby Colliery
58033	E	E	WFAN	TO	
58034	MG	E	WFAN	TO	Bassetlaw
58035	MG	E	WFAN	TO	
58036	ML	E	WFAN	TO	
58037	E	E	WFAN	TO	
58038	ML	E	WFAN	TO	
58039	E	E	WFAN	TO	
58040	MG	E	WFAN	TO	Cottam Power Station
58041	MG	E	WFAN	TO	Ratcliffe Power Station
58042	ML	E	WFAN	TO	Petrolea
58043	MG	E	WFAN	TO	
58044	MG	E	WFAN	TO	Oxcroft Opencast
58045	MG	E	WFAN	TO	
58046	ML	E	WFAN	TO	Asfordby Mine
58047	E	E	WFAN	TO	
58048	E	E	WFAN	TO	
58049	E	E	WFAN	TO	Littleton Colliery
58050	E	E	WFAN	TO	Toton Traction Depot

CLASS 59   GENERAL MOTORS   Co–Co

Built: 1985 (59001/002/004) or 1989 (59005) by General Motors, La Grange, Illinois, USA or 1990 (59101–4), 1994 (59201) and 1995 (59202–6) by General Motors, London, Ontario, Canada.
Engine: General Motors 645E3C two stroke of 2460 kW (3300 hp) at 900 rpm.
Main Alternator: General Motors AR11 MLD-D14A.
Traction Motors: General Motors D77B.
Max. Tractive Effort: 506 kN (113 550 lbf).
Cont. Tractive Effort: 291 kN (65 300 lbf) at 14.3 mph.
Power At Rail: 1889 kW (2533 hp).   **Train Brakes:** Air.
Brake Force: 69 t.   **Dimensions:** 21.35 x 2.65 x 3.9 m.
Weight: 121 t.   **Wheel Diameter:** 1067 mm.
Design Speed: 60 (* 75) mph.   **Max. Speed:** 60 (* 75) mph.
Fuel Capacity: 4546 litres.   **RA:** 7.
Train Supply: Not equipped.   **Multiple Working:** GM System.

Class 59/0. Owned by Foster-Yeoman Ltd.

59001	FY	FY	XYPO	MD	YEOMAN ENDEAVOUR
59002	FN	FY	XYPO	MD	ALAN J DAY
59004	FN	FY	XYPO	MD	PAUL A HAMMOND
59005	FY	FY	XYPO	MD	

Class 59/1. Owned by ARC Limited.

59101	**AC**	AC	XYPA	MD	Village of Whatley
59102	**AO**	AC	XYPA	MD	Village of Chantry
59103	**AO**	AC	XYPA	MD	Village of Mells
59104	**AO**	AC	XYPA	MD	Village of Great Elm

Class 59/2. Owned by English Welsh & Scottish Railway.

59201	*	**E**	E	WDAN	FB	Vale of York
59202	*	**E**	E	WDAN	FB	Vale of White Horse
59203	*	**E**	E	WDAN	FB	Vale of Pickering
59204	*	**E**	E	WDAN	FB	Vale of Glamorgan
59205	*	**E**	E	WDAN	FB	L. Keith McNair
59206	*	**E**	E	WDAN	FB	Pride of Ferrybridge

CLASS 60   BRUSH/MIRRLEES   Co–Co

Built: 1989–1993 by Brush Traction at Loughborough.
Engine: Mirrlees 8MB275T of 2310 kW (3100 hp) at 1000 rpm.
Main Alternator: Brush BA1000.
Traction Motors: Brush TM216.
Max. Tractive Effort: 500 kN (106500 lbf).
Cont. Tractive Effort: 336 kN (71570 lbf) at 17.4 mph.
Power At Rail: 1800 kW (2415 hp).   **Train Brakes:** Air.
Brake Force: 74 (+ 62) t.   **Dimensions:** 21.34 x 2.64 x 3.95 m.
Weight: 129 (+ 131) t.   **Wheel Diameter:** 1118 mm.
Design Speed: 62 mph.   **Max. Speed:** 60 mph.
Fuel Capacity: 4546 (+ 5225) litres.   **RA:** 7.
Train Supply: Not equipped.   **Multiple Working:** Within class.
Note: All equipped with Slow Speed Control.
Non-standard livery/numbering:
•   60006/033 are in British Steel livery of blue with white logos.
•   60064/070 are as **G**, with Loadhaul logos.

60001		**E**	E	WCAN	TO	
60002	+	**E**	E	WCAN	TO	High Peak
60003	+	**E**	E	WCAN	TO	FREIGHT TRANSPORT ASSOCIATION
60004	+	**E**	E	WCAN	TO	
60005	+	**E**	E	WCAN	TO	
60006		**O**	E	WCAN	TO	Scunthorpe Ironmaster
60007	+	**LH**	E	WCAN	TO	
60008		**LH**	E	WCAN	TO	GYPSUM QUEEN II
60009	+	**MG**	E	WCAN	TO	Carnedd Dafydd
60010	+	**E**	E	WCAN	TO	
60011		**ML**	E	WCAN	TO	
60012	+	**E**	E	WCAN	TO	
60013		**F**	E	WCAN	TO	Robert Boyle
60014		**FP**	E	WCAN	TO	Alexander Fleming
60015	+	**T**	E	WCAN	TO	Bow Fell
60016		**E**	E	WCAN	TO	
60017	+	**E**	E	WCAN	TO	Shotton Works Centenary Year 1996

60018		E	E	WCAN	TO	
60019		E	E	WCAN	TO	
60020	+	E	E	WCAN	TO	
60021	+	F	E	WCAN	TO	Pen-y-Ghent
60022	+	E	E	WCAN	TO	
60023	+	E	E	WCAN	TO	
60024	+	E	E	WCAN	TO	
60025	+	LH	E	WCAN	TO	
60026	+	E	E	WCAN	TO	
60027	+	E	E	WCAN	TO	
60028	+	E	E	WCAN	TO	John Flamsteed
60029		E	E	WCAN	TO	Clitheroe Castle
60030		E	E	WCAN	TO	
60031		FM	E	WCAN	TO	Ben Lui[1]
60032		T	E	WCAN	TO	William Booth
60033		O	E	WCAN	TO	Tees Steel Express
60034		T	E	WCAN	TO	Carnedd Llewelyn
60035		T	E	WCAN	TO	Florence Nightingale
60036		E	E	WCAN	TO	
60037	+	E	E	WCAN	TO	Aberthaw/Aberddawan
60038	+	LH	E	WCAN	TO	
60039		E	E	WCAN	TO	
60040		E	E	WCAN	TO	William Wilberforce[1]
60041	+	E	E	WCAN	TO	
60042	+	E	E	WCAN	TO	
60043		E	E	WCAN	TO	
60044		ML	E	WCAN	TO	Ailsa Craig
60045		E	E	WCAN	TO	The Permanent Way Institution
60046	+	T	E	WCAN	TO	William Wilberforce
60047	+	E	E	WCAN	TO	
60048		E	E	WCAN	TO	Eastern
60049	+	E	E	WCAN	TO	
60050	+	E	E	WCAN	TO	
60051	+	E	E	WCAN	TO	
60052	+	E	E	WCAN	TO	Glofa Twr The last deep mine in
						Wales Tower Colliery
60053	+	E	E	WCAN	TO	Nordic Terminal
60054	+	FP	E	WCAN	TO	Charles Babbage
60055		T	E	WCAN	TO	Thomas Barnardo
60056	+	T	E	WCAN	TO	William Beveridge
60057		FC	E	WCAN	TO	Adam Smith
60058		T	E	WCAN	TO	John Howard
60059	+	LH	E	WCAN	TO	Swinden Dalesman
60060		FC	E	WCAN	TO	James Watt
60061		T	E	WCAN	TO	Alexander Graham Bell
60062		T	E	WCAN	TO	Samuel Johnson
60063		T	E	WCAN	TO	James Murray
60064	+	O	E	WCAN	TO	Back Tor[1]
60065		T	E	WCAN	TO	Kinder Low
60066		FC	E	WCAN	TO	John Logie Baird
60067	+	F	E	WCAN	TO	James Clerk-Maxwell

60068	F	E	WCAN	TO	Charles Darwin
60069	F	E	WCAN	TO	Humphry Davy
60070	+ 0	E	WCAN	TO	John Loudon McAdam
60071	+ MG	E	WCAN	TO	Dorothy Garrod
60072	MG	E	WCAN	TO	Cairn Toul
60073	MG	E	WCAN	TO	Cairn Gorm[1]
60074	MG		WCAN	TO	Braeriach
60075	MG	E	WCAN	TO	
60076	MG	E	WCAN	TO	
60077	+ MG	E	WCAN	TO	Canisp[1]
60078	ML	E	WCAN	TO	
60079	MG	E	WCAN	TO	Foinaven
60080	+ T	E	WCAN	TO	Kinder Scout
60081	+ T	E	WCAN	TO	Bleaklow Hill[1]
60082	T	E	WCAN	TO	Mam Tor
60083	E	E	WCAN	TO	Mountsorrel
60084	T	E	WCAN	TO	Cross Fell
60085	T	E	WCAN	TO	
60086	MG	E	WCAN	TO	Schiehallion
60087	MG	E	WCAN	TO	Slioch
60088	MG	E	WCAN	TO	Buachaille Etive Mor
60089	T	E	WCAN	TO	Arcuil
60090	+ FC	E	WCAN	TO	Quinag
60091	+ FC	E	WCAN	TO	An Teallach
60092	F	E	WCAN	TO	Reginald Munns
60093	T	E	WCAN	TO	Jack Stirk
60094	MG	E	WCAN	TO	Tryfan
60095	F	E	WCAN	TO	
60096	+ T	E	WCAN	TO	Ben Macdui
60097	T	E	WCAN	TO	
60098	+ E	E	WCAN	TO	Charles Francis Brush
60099	MG	E	WCAN	TO	Ben More Assynt
60100	MG	E	WCAN	TO	Boar of Badenoch

CLASS 66   GENERAL MOTORS   Co–Co

Built: 1998–2000 by General Motors, London, Ontario, Canada (Model JT42CWR).
Engine: General Motors 12N-7103GB-EC two stroke of 2385 kW (3200 hp) at 900 rpm.
Main Alternator: General Motors AR8/C86.
Traction Motors: General Motors D43TR.
Max. Tractive Effort: 409 kN (92000 lbf).
Cont. Tractive Effort: 260 kN (53390 lbf) at 15.9 mph.

Power At Rail: 2236 (3000 hp) kW.	**Train Brakes:** Air.
Brake Force: 68 t.	**Dimensions:** 21.35 x 2.64 x 3.90 m.
Weight: 126 t.	**Wheel Diameter:** 1120 mm.
Design Speed: 75 mph.	**Max. Speed:** 75 mph.
Fuel Capacity: 6550 litres.	**RA:** 7.
Train Supply: Not equipped.	**Multiple Working:** GM System.

66001	E	A	WBAN	TO
66002	E	A	WBAN	TO
66003	E	A	WBAN	TO
66004	E	A	WBAN	TO
66005	E	A	WBAN	TO
66006	E	A	WBAN	TO
66007	E	A	WBAN	TO
66008	E	A	WBAN	TO
66009	E	A	WBAN	TO
66010	E	A	WBAN	TO
66011	E	A	WBAN	TO
66012	E	A	WBAN	TO
66013	E	A	WBAN	TO
66014	E	A	WBAN	TO
66015	E	A	WBAN	TO
66016	E	A	WBAN	TO
66017	E	A	WBAN	TO
66018	E	A	WBAN	TO
66019	E	A	WBAN	TO
66020	E	A	WBAN	TO
66021	E	A	WBAN	TO
66022	E	A	WBAN	TO
66023	E	A	WBAN	TO
66024	E	A	WBAN	TO
66025	E	A	WBAN	TO
66026	E	A	WBAN	TO
66027	E	A	WBAN	TO
66028	E	A	WBAN	TO
66029	E	A	WBAN	TO
66030	E	A	WBAN	TO
66031	E	A	WBAN	TO
66032	E	A	WBAN	TO
66033	E	A	WBAN	TO
66034		A	WBAN	
66035		A	WBAN	
66036		A	WBAN	
66037		A	WBAN	
66038		A	WBAN	
66039		A	WBAN	
66040		A	WBAN	
66041		A	WBAN	
66042		A	WBAN	
66043		A	WBAN	
66044		A	WBAN	
66045		A	WBAN	
66046		A	WBAN	
66047		A	WBAN	
66048		A	WBAN	
66049		A	WBAN	
66050		A	WBAN	
66051		A	WBAN	

66052	A	WBAN
66053	A	WBAN
66054	A	WBAN
66055	A	WBAN
66056	A	WBAN
66057	A	WBAN
66058	A	WBAN
66059	A	WBAN
66060	A	WBAN
66061	A	WBAN
66062	A	WBAN
66063	A	WBAN
66064	A	WBAN
66065	A	WBAN
66066	A	WBAN
66067	A	WBAN
66068	A	WBAN
66069	A	WBAN
66070	A	WBAN
66071	A	WBAN
66072	A	WBAN
66073	A	WBAN
66074	A	WBAN
66075	A	WBAN
66076	A	WBAN
66077	A	WBAN
66078	A	WBAN
66079	A	WBAN
66080	A	WBAN
66081	A	WBAN
66082	A	WBAN
66083	A	WBAN
66084	A	WBAN
66085	A	WBAN
66086	A	WBAN
66087	A	WBAN
66088	A	WBAN
66089	A	WBAN
66090	A	WBAN
66091	A	WBAN
66092	A	WBAN
66093	A	WBAN
66094	A	WBAN
66095	A	WBAN
66096	A	WBAN
66097	A	WBAN
66098	A	WBAN
66099	A	WBAN
66100	A	WBAN
66101	A	WBAN
66102	A	WBAN

66103	A	WBAN
66104	A	WBAN
66105	A	WBAN
66106	A	WBAN
66107	A	WBAN
66108	A	WBAN
66109	A	WBAN
66110	A	WBAN
66111	A	WBAN
66112	A	WBAN
66113	A	WBAN
66114	A	WBAN
66115	A	WBAN
66116	A	WBAN
66117	A	WBAN
66118	A	WBAN
66119	A	WBAN
66120	A	WBAN
66121	A	WBAN
66122	A	WBAN
66123	A	WBAN
66124	A	WBAN
66125	A	WBAN
66126	A	WBAN
66127	A	WBAN
66128	A	WBAN
66129	A	WBAN
66130	A	WBAN
66131	A	WBAN
66132	A	WBAN
66133	A	WBAN
66134	A	WBAN
66135	A	WBAN
66136	A	WBAN
66137	A	WBAN
66138	A	WBAN
66139	A	WBAN
66140	A	WBAN
66141	A	WBAN
66142	A	WBAN
66143	A	WBAN
66144	A	WBAN
66145	A	WBAN
66146	A	WBAN
66147	A	WBAN
66148	A	WBAN
66149	A	WBAN
66150	A	WBAN
66151	A	WBAN
66152	A	WBAN
66153	A	WBAN

66154	A	WBAN
66155	A	WBAN
66156	A	WBAN
66157	A	WBAN
66158	A	WBAN
66159	A	WBAN
66160	A	WBAN
66161	A	WBAN
66162	A	WBAN
66163	A	WBAN
66164	A	WBAN
66165	A	WBAN
66166	A	WBAN
66167	A	WBAN
66168	A	WBAN
66169	A	WBAN
66170	A	WBAN
66171	A	WBAN
66172	A	WBAN
66173	A	WBAN
66174	A	WBAN
66175	A	WBAN
66176	A	WBAN
66177	A	WBAN
66178	A	WBAN
66179	A	WBAN
66180	A	WBAN
66181	A	WBAN
66182	A	WBAN
66183	A	WBAN
66184	A	WBAN
66185	A	WBAN
66186	A	WBAN
66187	A	WBAN
66188	A	WBAN
66189	A	WBAN
66190	A	WBAN
66191	A	WBAN
66192	A	WBAN
66193	A	WBAN
66194	A	WBAN
66195	A	WBAN
66196	A	WBAN
66197	A	WBAN
66198	A	WBAN
66199	A	WBAN
66200	A	WBAN
66201	A	WBAN
66202	A	WBAN
66203	A	WBAN
66204	A	WBAN

66205	A	WBAN
66206	A	WBAN
66207	A	WBAN
66208	A	WBAN
66209	A	WBAN
66210	A	WBAN
66211	A	WBAN
66212	A	WBAN
66213	A	WBAN
66214	A	WBAN
66215	A	WBAN
66216	A	WBAN
66217	A	WBAN
66218	A	WBAN
66219	A	WBAN
66220	A	WBAN
66221	A	WBAN
66222	A	WBAN
66223	A	WBAN
66224	A	WBAN
66225	A	WBAN
66226	A	WBAN
66227	A	WBAN
66228	A	WBAN
66229	A	WBAN
66230	A	WBAN
66231	A	WBAN
66232	A	WBAN
66233	A	WBAN
66234	A	WBAN
66235	A	WBAN
66236	A	WBAN
66237	A	WBAN
66238	A	WBAN
66239	A	WBAN
66240	A	WBAN
66241	A	WBAN
66242	A	WBAN
66243	A	WBAN
66244	A	WBAN
66245	A	WBAN
66246	A	WBAN
66247	A	WBAN
66248	A	WBAN
66249	A	WBAN
66250	A	WBAN

CLASS 67   GENERAL MOTORS   Co–Co

Built: 1998–99 by Alstom at Valencia, Spain, as sub-contractors for General Motors.
Engine: General Motors 12N-7103GB-EC two stroke of 2385 kW (3200 hp) at 900 rpm.
Main Alternator: General Motors AR8/C86.
Traction Motors: General Motors D43TR.
Max. Tractive Effort:
Cont. Tractive Effort:
Power At Rail: 2236 (3000 hp) kW.
Brake Force:
Weight: 126 t.
Design Speed: 125 mph.
Fuel Capacity:
Train Supply: Electric.

Train Brakes: Air.
Dimensions: 21.02 x 2.72 x 3.95 m.
Wheel Diameter: 1120 mm.
Max. Speed: 125 mph.
RA:
Multiple Working: GM System.

67001	A	WAAN
67002	A	WAAN
67003	A	WAAN
67004	A	WAAN
67005	A	WAAN
67006	A	WAAN
67007	A	WAAN
67008	A	WAAN
67009	A	WAAN
67010	A	WAAN
67011	A	WAAN
67012	A	WAAN
67013	A	WAAN
67014	A	WAAN
67015	A	WAAN
67016	A	WAAN
67017	A	WAAN
67018	A	WAAN
67019	A	WAAN
67020	A	WAAN
67021	A	WAAN
67022	A	WAAN
67023	A	WAAN
67024	A	WAAN
67025	A	WAAN
67026	A	WAAN
67027	A	WAAN
67028	A	WAAN
67029	A	WAAN
67030	A	WAAN

1.2. ELECTRIC & ELECTRO-DIESEL LOCOMOTIVES

CLASS 71   BR/ENGLISH ELECTRIC   Bo–Bo

Built: 1959 by BR at Doncaster Works.
Electric Supply System: 750 V dc from third rail.
Traction Motors: English Electric 532.
Max. Tractive Effort: 195 kN (43800 lbf).
Continuous Rating: 1716 kW (2300 hp) giving a tractive effort of 55 kN (12400 lbf) at 69.6 mph.   **RA:** 6.
Maximum Rail Power: 2239 kW (3000 hp).
Train Brakes: Air, vacuum & electro-pneumatic.
Brake Force: 41 t.   **Dimensions:** 15.42 x 2.82 x 3.99 m.
Weight: 76.2 t.   **Wheel Diameter:** 1219 mm.
Design Speed: 90 mph   **Max. Speed:** 90 mph.
Train Supply: Electric (300 kW maximum).
Multiple Working: SR System.
Non-standard livery/numbering:
•   71001 carries number E5001.

71001   **G**   NR   MBEL   SE

CLASS 73   BR/ENGLISH ELECTRIC   Bo–Bo

Built: 1962 by BR at Eastleigh Works.
Engine: English Electric 4SRKT of 447 kW (600 hp) at 850 rpm.
Main Generator: English Electric 824/3D.
Electric Supply System: 750 V dc from third rail.
Traction Motors: English Electric 542A.
Max. Tractive Effort: Electric 187 kN (42000 lbf). Diesel 152 kN (34100 lbf).
Continuous Rating: Electric 1060 kW (1420 hp) giving a tractive effort of 43 kN (9600 lbf) at 55.5 mph.
Cont. Tractive Effort: Diesel 72 kN (16100 lbf) at 10 mph.
Maximum Rail Power: Electric 1830 kW (2450 hp) at 37 mph.
Train Brakes: Air, vacuum & electro-pneumatic († Air & electro-pneumatic).
Brake Force: 31 t.   **Dimensions:** 16.36 x 2.64 x 3.8 m.
Weight: 76.3 t.   **Wheel Diameter:** 1016 mm.
Design Speed: 80 mph   **Max. Speed:** 60 mph.
Fuel Capacity: 1545 litres.   **RA:** 6.
Train Supply: Electric, index 66 (on electric power only). May also deliver a reduced electric train supply when on diesel power whilst stationary.
Multiple Working: SR System.
Non-standard livery/numbering:
•   73005 is in non-standard blue livery with white roof.

Class 73/0. First build. Details as above.

| 73002 | **BL** | ME | HEBD | KK(S) |
| 73005 | **O** | ME | HEBD | BD |

Class 73/1. Later build. Revised details.

Built: 1965–67 by English Electric Co. at Vulcan Foundry, Newton le Willows.
Main Generator: English Electric 824/5D.
Traction Motors: English Electric 546/1B.
Max. Tractive Effort: Electric 179 kN (40000 lbf). Diesel 160 kN (36000 lbf).
Continuous Rating: Electric 1060 kW (1420 hp) giving a tractive effort of 35 kN (7800 lbf) at 68 mph.
Cont. Tractive Effort: Diesel 60 kN (13600 lbf) at 11.5 mph.
Maximum Rail Power: Electric 2350 kW (3150 hp) at 42 mph.
Weight: 77 t.   **Dimensions:** 16.36 x 2.64 x 3.81m.
Design Speed: 90 mph.   **Max. Speed:** 60 (90*) mph.
Fuel Capacity: 1409 litres.
Train Supply: Electric, index 66 (on electric power only).
Note: ‡ Modified cabs for use on route learning duties.

73101	*	**PC**	E	WPAN	HG	The Royal Alex'
73103		**I**	E	WPAN	HG	
73104	*	**I**	E	WPAN	HG	
73105	*	**CE**	E	WPAN	HG	
73106		**DG**	E	WPAN	HG	
73107	*	**CE**	E	WPAN	HG	Redhill 1844-1994
73108		**E**	E	WPAN	HG	
73109	*	**ST**	SW	HYSB	BM	Battle of Britain 50th Anniversary
73110		**CE**	E	WPAN	HG	
73114	*	**ML**	E	WPAN	HG	Stewarts Lane Traction Maintenance Depot
73117		**I**	E	WPAN	HG	University of Surrey
73118	†c	**EU**	EU	GPSN	OC	
73119	*	**CE**	E	WPAN	HG	Kentish Mercury
73126		**N**	E	WNYX	OC(S)	
73128	*	**E**	E	WPAR	HG	
73129	*	**N**	E	WPAN	HG	City of Winchester
73130	†c	**EU**	EU	GPSN	OC	
73131	*	**E**	E	WPAR	HG	
73132		**I**	E	WNXX	HG(S)	
73133	‡	**ML**	E	WPAN	HG	The Bluebell Railway
73134		**I**	E	WPAN	HG	Woking Homes 1885-1985
73136		**ML**	E	WPAN	HG	Kent Youth Music
73138		**CE**	E	WPAN	HG	
73139		**I**	E	WPAR	HG	
73140		**I**	E	WNXX	OC(S)	
73141		**I**	E	WPAR	HG	

Class 73/2. Gatwick Express locomotives. Details as Class 73/1 except:
Max. Speed: 90 mph.   **Train Brakes:** Air & electro-pneumatic.

| 73201 | **GX** | GX | IVGA | SL | Broadlands |
| 73202 | **GX** | GX | IVGA | SL | Royal Observer Corps |

73203	**GX**	GX	IVGA	SL	
73204	**GX**	GX	IVGA	SL	Stewarts Lane 1860-1985
73205	**GX**	GX	IVGA	SL	
73206	**GX**	GX	IVGA	SL	Gatwick Express
73207	**GX**	GX	IVGA	SL	County of East Sussex
73208	**GX**	GX	IVGA	SL	Croydon 1883-1983
73209	**GX**	GX	IVGA	SL	
73210	**GX**	GX	IVGA	SL	Selhurst
73211	**GX**	GX	IVGA	SL	
73212	**GX**	GX	IVGA	SL	Airtour Suisse
73213	**GX**	GX	IVGA	SL	University of Kent at Canterbury
73235	**GX**	GX	IVGA	SL	

**Class 73/9. Merseyrail Electrics engineering and sandite train locomotives.
Details as Class 73/0.**

73901	**MD**	ME	HEBD	BD
73906	**MD**	ME	HEBD	BD

NOTES FOR CLASSES 86–91

The following common features apply to all locos of Classes 86–91.

Supply System: 25 kV a.c. 50 Hz overhead.
Multiple Working: Time division multiplex system.

CLASS 86   BR/ENGLISH ELECTRIC   Bo–Bo

Built: 1965–66 by English Electric Co. at Vulcan Foundry, Newton le Willows
or by BR at Doncaster Works.
Traction Motors: AEI 282BZ frame mounted.
Max. Tractive Effort: 207 kN (46500 lbf).
Continuous Rating: 3010 kW (4040 hp) giving a tractive effort of 85 kN (19200
lbf) at 77.5 mph.
Maximum Rail Power: 4550 kW (6100 hp) at 49.5 mph.
Train Brakes: Air.
Brake Force: 40 t.   **Dimensions:** 17.83 x 2.65 x 3.98
m.Weight: 83–86.8 t.   **Wheel Diameter:** 1156 mm.**Design**
Speed: 100 mph.   **Max. Speed:** 100 mph
Train Supply: Electric, index 74.   **RA:** 6.

Class 86/1. Class 87 type bogies and motors. Details as above except:
Max. Tractive Effort: 258 kN (58000 lbf).
Traction Motors: GEC 412AZ.
Continuous Rating: 3730 kW (5000 hp) giving a TE of 95 kN (21300 lbf) at 87 mph.
Maximum Rail Power: 5860 kW (7860 hp) at 50.8 mph.
Weight: 86.8 t.   **Wheel Diameter:** 1150 mm.
Design Speed: 110 mph   **Max. Speed:** 110 mph.

86101		**IS**	F	WEMF	CE	Sir William A Stanier FRS
86102		**IS**	F	WEMF	CE	Robert A Riddles
86103	x	**IS**	F	SAXL	CE(S)	André Chapelon

Class 86/2. Standard Design. Details as in main class heading except:
Weight: 85–86.2 t.
Non-standard livery/numbering:
    86245 is as **V**, but with blue replacing red as the main colour and red
    rather than white stripes.

86204		IS	F	SAXL	ZH(S)	City of Carlisle
86205		IS	F	SAXL	CE(S)	City of Lancaster
86206		IS	F	SAXL	LB(S)	City of Stoke on Trent
86207		IS	F	SAXL	ZH(S)	City of Lichfield
86208		IS	E	WEMP	CE	City of Chester
86209		IS	F	SAXL	ZH(S)	City of Coventry
86210	x	RX	E	WEMP	CE	C.I.T. 75th Anniversary
86212		IS	F	ICCA	LG	Preston Guild 1328-1992
86213		IS	F	SAXL	ZH(S)	Lancashire Witch
86214		IS	F	ICCA	LG	Sans Pareil
86215		AR	F	IANA	NC	Norwich & Norfolk Festival
86216		IS	F	SAXL	ZH(S)	Meteor
86217		IS	F	IANA	NC	City University
86218		AR	F	IANA	NC	NHS 50
86219		IS	F	SAXL	ZH(S)	Phoenix
86220		IS	F	IANA	NC	The Round Tabler
86221		IS	F	IANA	NC	B.B.C. Look East
86222		IS	F	ICCA	LG	Clothes Show Live
86223		IS	F	IANA	NC	Norwich Union
86224		IS	F	ICCA	LG	
86225		IS	F	ICCA	LG	Hardwicke
86226		IS	F	ICCA	LG	CHARLES RENNIE MACKINTOSH
86227		IS	F	SAXL	LG(S)	Sir Henry Johnson
86228		IS	F	IANA	NC	Vulcan Heritage
86229		V	F	IWPA	WN	Lions Clubs International
86230		IS	F	IANA	NC	
86231		IS	F	ICCA	LG	Starlight Express
86232		IS	F	IANA	NC	
86233		IS	F	IWPA	WN	Laurence Olivier
86234		IS	F	SAXL	ZH(S)	J B Priestley OM
86235		IS	F	IANA	NC	Crown Point
86236		IS	F	ICCA	LG	Josiah Wedgwood MASTER POTTER 1736-1795
86237		IS	F	IANA	NC	University of East Anglia
86238		IS	F	IANA	NC	European Community
86240		IS	F	ICCA	LG	Bishop Eric Treacy
86241		RX	E	WEMP	CE	Glenfiddich
86242		V	F	ICCA	LG	James Kennedy GC
86243	x	RX	E	WEMP	CE	
86244		IS	F	ICCA	LG	The Royal British Legion
86245		O	F	IWPA	WN	Caledonian
86246		AR	F	IANA	NC	Royal Anglian Regiment
86247		IS	F	IWPA	WN	Abraham Darby
86248		IS	F	ICCA	LG	Sir Clwyd/County of Clwyd
86249		IS	F	SAXL	ZH(S)	County of Merseyside

86250		**AR**	F	IANA	NC	
86251		**IS**	F	ICCA	LG	The Birmingham Post
86252		**IS**	F	IANA	NC	The Liverpool Daily Post
86253		**IS**	F	IANA	NC	The Manchester Guardian
86254	x	**RX**	E	WEMP	CE	
86255		**IS**	F	SAXL	LG(S)	Penrith Beacon
86256		**IS**	F	ICCA	LG	Pebble Mill
86257		**AR**	F	IANA	NC	Snowdon
86258		**IS**	F	ICCA	LG	Talyllyn-The First Preserved Railway
86259		**IS**	F	IWPA	WN	Greater MANCHESTER THE LIFE &
						SOUL OF BRITAIN
86260		**IS**	F	IWPA	WN	Driver Wallace Oakes G.C.
86261	x	**E**	E	WEMP	CE	THE RAIL CHARTER PARTNERSHIP

Class 86/4. EWS (Rail Express Systems) locomotives. Details as Class 86/2 except:
Max. Tractive Effort: 258 kN (58000 lbf).
Traction Motors: AEI 412AZ.   **Weight:** 83–83.9 t.
Continuous Rating: 2680 kW (3600 hp) giving a tractive effort of 89 kN (20000 lbf) at 67 mph.
Maximum Rail Power: 4400 kW (5900 hp) at 38 mph.

86401		**E**	E	WEMP	CE	
86416	x	**RX**	E	WEMP	CE	Hertfordshire Railtours
86417	x	**RX**	E	WEMP	CE	
86419	x	**RX**	E	WEMP	CE	
86424	x	**RX**	E	WEMP	CE	
86425	x	**RX**	E	WEMF	CE	Saint Mungo
86426	x	**E**	E	WEMP	CE	Pride of the Nation
86430	x	**RX**	E	WEMP	CE	Saint Edmund

Class 86/6. Freightliner locomotives. Details as Class 86/4 except:
Max. Speed: 75 mph.   **Train Supply:** Electric, isolated.

86602		**F**	FL	DFNC	CE	
86603		**FE**	FL	DFNC	CE	
86604		**FF**	FL	DFNC	CE	
86605		**FF**	FL	DFNC	CE	
86606		**FF**	FL	DFNC	CE	
86607		**F**	FL	DFNC	CE	The Institution of Electrical Engineers
86608		**FE**	FL	DFNC	CE	St John Ambulance
86609		**F**	FL	DFNC	CE	
86610		**F**	FL	DFNC	CE	
86611		**FF**	FL	DFNC	CE	Airey Neave
86612		**FF**	P	DFNC	CE	Elizabeth Garrett Anderson
86613		**FF**	P	DFNC	CE	County of Lancashire
86614		**FF**	P	DFNC	CE	Frank Hornby
86615		**F**	P	DFNC	CE	Rotary International
86618		**FF**	P	DFNC	CE	
86620		**FL**	P	DFNC	CE	Philip G Walton
86621		**FF**	P	DFNC	CE	London School of Economics
86622		**FF**	P	DFNC	CE	
86623		**FF**	P	DFNC	CE	

▲ Freightliner's 57001 takes on fuel at the company's recently opened fuelling point at Crewe Basford Hall Yard on 17th August 1998.   **Neil Webster**

▼ Mainline blue liveried 58021 'Hither Green Depot' stands, appropriately, at Hither Green depot on 14th May 1998.   **Rodney Lissenden**

▲ All the Class 59/2 locomotives acquired by EWS from National Power have now been repainted in EWS corporate livery. 59203 'Vale of Pickering', is seen here at Knottingley at the head of a Drax–Milford empty wagon train on 4th September 1998. **Michael J. Collins**

▼ Transrail liveried 60061 'Alexander Graham Bell' passes through the industrial landscape of Widnes with a train of empty 'merry-go-round' hoppers en route to Gladstone Dock on 24th September 1997. **Nic Joynson**

English Welsh & Scottish Railway is receiving deliveries of its order for 250 Class 66 locomotives from General Motors in Canada at quite a fast pace. 66001 was exhibited at Foster Yeoman's 75th anniversary event at Merehead on 27th June 1998.

Hugh Ballantyne

▲ With both loco and coaches looking in smart in Gatwick Express corporate livery, 73205 passes Horley with the 16.30 London Victoria–Gatwick Airport on 9th May 1998.　　　　　　　　　　　　　　　　　　　　　**Nic Joynson**

▼ In its 'home' county, 87025 'County of Cheshire' passes Red Bank, near Winwick Junction with the 11.20 Preston–London Euston on 15th May 1997.　　**Nic Joynson**

Anglia Railways 86215, then un-named but now named 'Norfolk & Norwich Festival' passes Stratford with the 10.05 Norwich–London Liverpool Street on 17th September 1998. **Brian Denton**

▲ Unique 89001 operates on a self-contained diagram between London King's Cross and Leeds. It is seen here awaiting departure time at King's Cross at the head of the 07.50 'Yorkshire Pullman' on 8th May 1998. **Hugh Ballantyne**

▼ Railfreight Distribution liveried 90134 departs from Wembley Yard with the 13.08 Dagenham Dock–Mossend Yard on 21st May 1998. **Brian Denton**

▲ 91014 approaches Doncaster with the 10.00 London King's Cross–Glasgow Central on 19th August 1998. **Les Nixon**

▼ Eurotunnel 'Shuttle' loco 9024 arrives at the UK terminal at Cheriton with a car shuttle on 17th May 1997. **Hugh Ballantyne**

92023 'Ravel' passes Kemsing with the 09.33 Wembley–Dollands Moor freight on 24th March 1998.   **Rodney Lissenden**

86627	F	P	DFNC	CE	The Industrial Society
86628	FF	P	DFNC	CE	Aldaniti
86631	FL	P	DFNC	CE	
86632	F	P	DFNC	CE	Brookside
86633	FF	P	DFNC	CE	Wulfruna
86634	F	P	DFNC	CE	University of London
86635	F	P	DFNC	CE	
86636	F	P	DFNC	CE	
86637	FF	P	DFNC	CE	
86638	FF	P	DFNC	CE	
86639	FF	P	DFNC	CE	

CLASS 87   BREL/GEC   Bo–Bo

Built: 1973–75 by BREL at Crewe Works.
Traction Motors: GEC G412AZ frame mounted.
Max. Tractive Effort: 258 kN (58000 lbf).
Continuous Rating: 3730 kW (5000 hp) giving a TE of 95 kN (21300 lbf) at 87 mph.
Maximum Rail Power: 5860 kW (7860 hp) at 50.8 mph.
Train Brakes: Air.
Brake Force: 40 t.
Weight: 83.3 t.
Design Speed: 110 mph
Train Supply: Electric, index 95 (* 66).

Dimensions: 17.83 x 2.65 x 3.96 m.
Wheel Diameter: 1150 mm.
Max. Speed: 110 mph
RA: 6.

Class 87/0. Standard Design.

87001		IS	P	IWCA	WN	Royal Scot
87002		IS	P	IWCA	WN	Royal Sovereign
87003		V	P	IWCA	WN	Patriot
87004		V	P	IWCA	WN	Britannia
87005		IS	P	IWCA	WN	City of London
87006		V	P	IWCA	WN	George Reynolds
87007		IS	P	IWCA	WN	
87008		V	P	IWCA	WN	
87009	*	V	P	IWCA	WN	
87010		IS	P	IWCA	WN	King Arthur
87011		IS	P	IWCA	WN	
87012		V	P	IWCA	WN	
87013		V	P	IWCA	WN	
87014		IS	P	IWCA	WN	Knight of the Thistle
87015		IS	P	IWCA	WN	Howard of Effingham
87016		V	P	IWCA	WN	Willesden Intercity Depot
87017		IS	P	IWCA	WN	Iron Duke
87018		IS	P	IWCA	WN	Lord Nelson
87019		IS	P	IWCA	WN	Sir Winston Churchill
87020		IS	P	IWCA	WN	North Briton
87021		IS	P	IWCA	WN	Robert The Bruce
87022		V	P	IWCA	WN	Lew Adams The Black Prince
87023		IS	P	IWCA	WN	Velocity
87024		IS	P	IWCA	WN	Lord of the Isles

87025	**V**	P	IWCA	WN	County of Cheshire
87026	**IS**	P	IWCA	WN	Sir Richard Arkwright
87027	**IS**	P	IWCA	WN	Wolf of Badenoch
87028	**IS**	P	IWCA	WN	Lord President
87029 *	**IS**	P	IWCA	WN	Earl Marischal
87030	**IS**	P	IWCA	WN	Black Douglas
87031	**IS**	P	IWCA	WN	Hal o' the Wynd
87032	**V**	P	IWCA	WN	Kenilworth
87033	**IS**	P	IWCA	WN	Thane of Fife
87034	**IS**	P	IWCA	WN	William Shakespeare
87035	**IS**	P	IWCA	WN	Robert Burns

Class 87/1. Thyristor Control. Details as Class 87/0 except:

Traction Motors: GEC G412BZ frame mounted.
Continuous Rating: 3620 kW (4850 hp) giving a TE of 96 kN (21600 lbf) at 84 mph.
Max. Speed: 75 mph.

| 87101 | **B** | E | WEMF | CE | Stephenson |

CLASS 89   BRUSH   Co–Co

Built: 1986 by BREL at Crewe Works (as sub-contractors for Brush).
Traction Motors: Brush. Frame mounted.
Max. Tractive Effort: 205 kN (46000 lbf).
Continuous Rating: 4350 kW (5850 hp) giving a TE of 105 kN (23600 lbf) at 92 mph.

Maximum Rail Power:	**Train Brakes:** Air.
Brake Force: 50 t.	**Dimensions:** 19.80 x 2.74 x 3.98 m.
Weight: 104 t.	**Wheel Diameter:** 1150 mm.
Design Speed: 125 mph	**Max. Speed:** 125 mph.
Train Supply: Electric, index 95.	**RA:** 6.

| 89001 | **GN** | SS | IECB | BN |

CLASS 90   GEC   Bo–Bo

Built: 1987–90 by BREL at Crewe Works (as sub contractors for GEC).
Traction Motors: GEC G412CY frame mounted.
Max. Tractive Effort: 258 kN (58000 lbf).
Continuous Rating: 3730 kW (5000 hp) giving a TE of 95 kN (21300 lbf) at 87 mph.
Maximum Rail Power: 5860 kW (7860 hp) at 68.3 mph.
Train Brakes: Air.

Brake Force: 40 t.	**Dimensions:** 18.80 x 2.74 x 3.97 m.
Weight: 84.5 t.	**Wheel Diameter:** 1156 mm.
Design Speed: 110 mph	**Max. Speed:** 110 mph.
Train Supply: Electric, index 95.	**RA:** 7.

Note: 90025–90029 were renumbered from 90125–129 respectively in 1998.
Non-standard liveries/numbering:
* 90028 is in Belgian National Railways style blue and yellow.
* 90029 is in German Federal Railways style red and white.
* 90130 is in French National Railways style two-tone grey.
* 90136 is as **FD**, but has a yellow roof.

Class 90/0. Standard Design. Details as above.

90001	**IS**	P	IWCA	WN	BBC Midlands Today
90002	**V**	P	IWCA	WN	Mission: Impossible
90003	**IS**	P	IWCA	WN	THE HERALD
90004	**V**	P	IWCA	WN	
90005	**IS**	P	IWCA	WN	Financial Times
90006	**IS**	P	IWCA	WN	High Sheriff
90007	**IS**	P	IWCA	WN	Lord Stamp
90008	**IS**	P	IWCA	WN	The Birmingham Royal Ballet
90009	**IS**	P	IWCA	WN	
90010	**IS**	P	IWCA	WN	275 Railway Squadron (Volunteers)
90011	**IS**	P	IWCA	WN	The Chartered Institute of Transport
90012	**V**	P	IWCA	WN	British Transport Police
90013	**IS**	P	IWCA	WN	The Law Society
90014	**V**	P	IWCA	WN	The Big Dish
90015	**V**	P	IWCA	WN	The International Brigades SPAIN 1936-1939
90016	**RX**	E	WEMP	CE	
90017	**RX**	E	WEMP	CE	Rail Express Systems Quality Assured
90018	**RX**	E	WEMP	CE	
90019	**RX**	E	WEMP	CE	
90020	**E**	E	WEMP	CE	Sir Michael Heron
90021	**FE**	E	WEMP	CE	
90022	**FE**	E	WEMP	CE	Freightconnection
90023	**FE**	E	WEMP	CE	
90024	**FE**	E	WEMP	CE	
90025	**FD**	E	WEMF	CE	
90026	**FE**	E	WEMP	CE	Crewe International Electric Maintenance Depot
90027	**FD**	E	WEMF	CE	Allerton T & RS Depot Quality Approved
90028	**O**	E	WEMP	CE	Vrachtverbinding
90029	**O**	E	WEMF	CE	Frachtverbindungen

Class 90/1. EWS & Freightliner locomotives. Details as Class 90/0 except:
Max. Speed: 75 mph.   **Train Supply**: Electric, isolated.

90130	**O**	E	WEMF	CE	Fretconnection
90131	**FE**	E	WEMF	CE	Intercontainer
90132	**FE**	E	WEMF	CE	Cerestar
90133	**FE**	E	WEMF	CE	
90134	**FE**	E	WEMF	CE	
90135	**FE**	E	WEMF	CE	Crewe Basford Hall
90136	**O**	E	WEMF	CE	
90137	**FD**	E	WEMF	CE	
90138	**FE**	E	WEMF	CE	
90139	**FD**	E	WEMF	CE	
90140	**FD**	E	WEMF	CE	
90141	**FF**	P	DFLC	CE	
90142	**FF**	P	DFLC	CE	
90143	**FF**	P	DFLC	CE	Freightliner Coatbridge

90144	**FF**	P	DFLC	CE
90145	**FF**	P	DFLC	CE
90146	**FF**	P	DFLC	CE
90147	**FF**	P	DFLC	CE
90148	**FF**	P	DFLC	CE
90149	**FF**	P	DFLC	CE
90150	**FF**	P	DFLC	CE

CLASS 91   GEC   Bo–B

Built: 1988–91 by BREL at Crewe Works (as sub contractors for GEC).
Traction Motors: GEC G426AZ.
Continuous Rating: 4540 kW (6090 hp).
Maximum Rail Power: 4700 kW (6300 hp).
Train Brakes: Air.
Brake Force: 45 t.   **Dimensions:** 19.41 x 2.74 x 3.76 m.
Weight: 84 t.   **Wheel Diameter:** 1000 mm.
Design Speed: 140 mph.   **Max. Speed:** 125 mph.
Train Supply: Electric, index 95.   **RA:** 7.

91001	**GN**	F	IECA	BN	
91002	**GN**	F	IECA	BN	
91003	**GN**	F	IECA	BN	
91004	**GN**	F	IECA	BN	
91005	**GN**	F	IECA	BN	
91006	**GN**	F	IECA	BN	
91007	**GN**	F	IECA	BN	
91008	**GN**	F	IECA	BN	
91009	**GN**	F	IECA	BN	The Samaritans
91010	**GN**	F	IECA	BN	
91011	**GN**	F	IECA	BN	
91012	**GN**	F	IECA	BN	
91013	**GN**	F	IECA	BN	
91014	**GN**	F	IECA	BN	
91015	**GN**	F	IECA	BN	
91016	**GN**	F	IECA	BN	
91017	**GN**	F	IECA	BN	
91018	**GN**	F	IECA	BN	
91019	**GN**	F	IECA	BN	
91020	**GN**	F	IECA	BN	
91021	**GN**	F	IECA	BN	
91022	**GN**	F	IECA	BN	
91023	**GN**	F	IECA	BN	
91024	**GN**	F	IECA	BN	
91025	**GN**	F	IECA	BN	
91026	**GN**	F	IECA	BN	
91027	**GN**	F	IECA	BN	
91028	**GN**	F	IECA	BN	
91029	**GN**	F	IECA	BN	
91030	**GN**	F	IECA	BN	
91031	**GN**	F	IECA	BN	

CLASS 92   BRUSH   Co–Co

Built: 1993–96 by Brush Traction at Loughborough.
Supply System: 25 kV a.c. 50 HZ overhead and 750 V d.c. third rail.
Traction Motors: Brush.
Max. Tractive Effort: 400 kN (90 000 lbf).
Continuous Rating: 5040 kW (6760 hp) on a.c, 4000 kW (5360 hp) on d.c.
Maximum Rail Power: **Train Brakes:** Air.
Brake Force: 63 t.   **Dimensions:** 21.34 x ?? x ?? m.
Weight: 126 t.   **Wheel Diameter:** 1160 mm.
Design Speed: 140 km/h (87½ mph). **Max. Speed:** 140 km/h (87½ mph).
Train Supply: Electric, index 108 (ac), 70 (dc).   **RA:** 8.
Multiple Working: Time division multiplex system.

92001	E	E	WTWN	CE	Victor Hugo
92002	EU	E	WTAN	CE	H.G. Wells
92003	EU	E	WTAN	CE	Beethoven
92004	EU	E	WTAN	CE	Jane Austen
92005	EU	E	WTAN	CE	Mozart
92006	EU	SF	WTAN	CE	Louis Armand
92007	EU	E	WTAN	CE	Schubert
92008	EU	E	WTWN	CE	Jules Verne
92009	EU	E	WTAN	CE	Elgar
92010	EU	SF	WTAN	CE	Molière
92011	EU	E	WTAN	CE	Handel
92012	EU	E	WTWN	CE	Thomas Hardy
92013	EU	E	WTWN	CE	Puccini
92014	EU	SF	WTAN	CE	Emile Zola
92015	EU	E	WTAN	CE	D.H. Lawrence
92016	EU	E	WTAN	CE	Brahms
92017	EU	E	WTAN	CE	Shakespeare
92018	EU	SF	WTAN	CE	Stendhal
92019	EU	E	WTWN	CE	Wagner
92020	EU	EU	WTAN	CE	Milton
92021	EU	EU	WTAN	CE	Purcell
92022	EU	E	WTAN	CE	Charles Dickens
92023	EU	SF	WTAN	CE	Ravel
92024	EU	E	WTWN	CE	J.S. Bach
92025	EU	E	WTAN	CE	Oscar Wilde
92026	EU	E	WTAN	CE	Britten
92027	EU	E	WTAN	CE	George Eliot
92028	EU	SF	WTAN	CE	Saint Saëns
92029	EU	E	WTAN	CE	Dante
92030	EU	E	WTAN	CE	Ashford
92031	EU	E	WTAN	CE	
92032	EU	EU	WTAN	CE	César Franck
92033	EU	SF	WTAN	CE	Berlioz
92034	EU	E	WTWN	CE	Kipling
92035	EU	E	WTAN	CE	Mendelssohn
92036	EU	E	WTAN	CE	Bertolt Brecht
92037	EU	E	WTWN	CE	Sullivan

92038	**EU**	SF	WTAN	CE	Voltaire
92039	**EU**	E	WTAN	CE	Johann Strauss
92040	**EU**	EU	WTAN	CE	Goethe
92041	**EU**	E	WTAN	CE	Vaughan Williams
92042	**EU**	E	WTAN	CE	Honegger
92043	**EU**	SF	WTAN	CE	Debussy
92044	**EU**	EU	WTAN	CE	Couperin
92045	**EU**	EU	WTAN	CE	Chaucer
92046	**EU**	EU	WTAN	CE	Sweelinck

1.3. MISCELLANEOUS VEHICLES

POWER UNIT TRANSPORTER/MAINTENANCE VEHICLE

Built: 1962-63 by English Electric Company at Vulcan Foundry, Newton le Willows (025031) or by Robert Stephenson & Hawthorn at Darlington (025032) as Class 37 locomotives. Converted to present use 1996 at Toton depot. Also carry local numbers 1 & 2 respectively.

| 025031 (37070) | **DG** | E | | TO |
| 025032 (37138) | **DG** | E | | TO |

1.4. LOCOMOTIVES AWAITING DISPOSAL

Included in this section are locomotives awaiting disposal of classes which do not otherwise feature in this publication.

Class 25

| 25083 | **B** | E | WNZX | CP(S) |

Class 45

| 45015 | **B** | E | WNZX | TT(S) |

2. EUROTUNNEL LOCOMOTIVES

Depot: Coquelles (France).

0001–0005   MAK   Bo-Bo

Built: 1992–93 by MaK at Kiel, Germany (Model DE1004).
Engine: MTU 12V 396 Tc of 1180 kW (1580 hp) at 1800 rpm.
Main Alternator: BBC.   **Traction Motors:** BBC.
Max. Tractive Effort: 305 kN (68600 lbf).
Cont. Tractive Effort: 140 kN (31500 lbf) at 20 mph.
Power At Rail: 750 kW (1012 hp).
Brake Force: 120 kN.   **Dimensions:** 16.50 x ?? x ?? m.
Weight: 84 t.   **Wheel Diameter:** 1000 mm.
Design Speed: 120 km/h.   **Max. Speed:** 120 km/h.
Fuel Capacity: **Train Brakes:** Air.
Train Supply: Not equipped.   **Multiple Working:** Within class.
Livery: Grey and yellow.

| 0001 | 0002 | 0003 | 0004 | 0005 |

0032–0042   HUNSLET/SCHÖMA   0-4-0

Built: 1989–90 by Hunslet Engine Company at Leeds as 900 mm. gauge.
Rebuilt: 1993-94 by Schöma in Germany as 1435 mm. gauge.
Engine: Deutz of 270 kW (200 hp) at ???? rpm.
Transmission: Mechanical.   **Max. Tractive Effort:**
Cont. Tractive Effort: **Power At Rail:**
Brake Force: **Dimensions:**
Weight: **Wheel Diameter:**
Design Speed: 50 km/h.   **Max. Speed:** 50 km/h.
Fuel Capacity: **Train Brakes:** Air.
Train Supply: Not equipped.   **Multiple Working:** Not equipped.
Livery: Plain yellow.

0031	FRANCES	0037	LYDIE
0032	ELISABETH	0038	JENNY
0033	SILKE	0039	PACITA
0034	AMANDA	0040	JILL
0035	MARY	0041	KIM
0036	LAWRENCE	0042	NICOLE

9001–9105   BRUSH/ABB   Bo-Bo-Bo

Built: 1993–99 by Brush Traction at Loughborough. 9040 and 9105 remained
to be delivered at the time of going to press.
Supply System: 25 kV a.c. 50 Hz overhead.
Traction Motors: ABB 6PH.   **Max. Tractive Effort:** 400 kN (90 000 lbf).
Continuous Rating: 5760 kW (7725 hp) giving a TE of 310 kN at 65 km/h.

Maximum Rail Power:
Brake Force: 50 t.   **Dimensions:** 22.00 x ?? x ?? m.
Weight: 132 t.   **Wheel Diameter:** 1090 mm.
Design Speed: 175 km/h.   **Max. Speed:** 160 km/h.
Train Supply: Electric.   **Train Brakes:** Air.
Multiple Working: Time division multiplex system.

9001	LESLEY GARRETT
9002	STUART BURROWS
9003	BENJAMIN LUXON
9004	VICTORIA DE LOS ANGELES
9005	JESSYE NORMAN
9006	REGINE CRISPIN
9007	DAME JOAN SUTHERLAND
9008	ELISABETH SODERSTROM
9009	FRANÇOISE POLLET
9010	JEAN-PHILLIPE COURTIS
9011	JOSÉ VAN DAM
9012	LUCIANO PAVAROTTI
9013	MARIA CALLAS
9014	LUCIA POPP
9015	LÖTSCHBERG
9016	WILLARD WHITE
9017	JOSÉ CARRERAS
9018	WILHELMENA FERNANDEZ
9019	EMARIA EWING
9020	NICOLAI GHIAROV
9021	THERESA BERGANZA
9022	DAME JANET BAKER
9023	DAME ELIZABETH LEGGE-SCHWARZKOPF
9024	GOTTHARD 1882
9025	JUNGFRAUJOCH
9026	FURKATUNNEL
9027	BARBARA HENDRICKS
9028	DAME KIRI TE KANAWA
9029	THOMAS ALLEN
9031	PLACIDO DOMINGO
9032	RENATA TEBALDI
9033	MONTSERRAT CABALLE
9034	MIRELLA FRENI
9035	NICOLAI GEDDA
9036	ALAIN FONDARY
9037	GABRIEL BACQUIER
9038	HILDEGARD BEHRENS
9040	
9101	
9102	
9103	
9104	
9105	

3. LIVERY CODES

Code	Description
AC	ARC *(Yellow/silver. Cast numberplates)*.
AO*	ARC *(Mustard with grey cabsides. Cast numberplates)*.
AR	Anglia Railways *(Turquoise blue with white stripe)*.
B*	BR *(Blue)*.
BL*	BR *(Blue with yellow cabs, grey roof, large numbers)*.
BR*	BR *(Blue with red solebar stripe)*.
CE*	BR Civil Engineers *(Yellow & grey with black cab doors and window surrounds)*.
DG*	BR Departmental *(Plain dark grey with black cab doors and window surrounds)*.
DR	Direct Rail Services *(Dark blue with light blue roof)*.
E	English Welsh & Scottish Railway *(Maroon bodyside & roof with gold stripe, gold reflective stripe at solebar level)*.
EP	European Passenger Services *(Two-tone grey with dark blue roof)*.
ET	Eurotunnel *(Two-tone grey and white with green and blue bands)*.
F*	BR Trainload Freight *(Two-tone grey with black cab doors and window surrounds. No logos)*.
FA*	BR Trainload Construction *(Two-tone grey with black cab doors and window surrounds. Yellow & blue chequered logo)*.
FC*	BR Trainload Coal *(Two-tone grey with black cab doors and window surrounds. Black & yellow logo)*.
FD*	BR Railfreight Distribution *(Two-tone grey with black cab doors and window surrounds. Yellow & red logo)*.
FE*	Railfreight Distribution International *(Two tone-grey with black cab doors and dark blue roof. Red & yellow logo)*.
FF	Freightliner *(Two-tone grey with black cab doors and window surrounds. Freightliner logo)*.
FG	Fragonset Railways *(Black with silver roof and a red bodyside band lined out in white)*.
FL	Freightliner *(Dark green with yellow cabs)*
FM*	BR Trainload Metals *(Two-tone grey with black cab doors and window surrounds. Yellow & blue chevrons logo)*.
FN*	Foster Yeoman *(Blue/silver/blue. Cast numberplates)*.
FO*	BR Railfreight *(Grey bodyside, yellow cabs, red buffer beam, large double-arrow logo)*.
FP*	BR Trainload Petroleum *(Two-tone grey with black cab doors and window surrounds. Yellow & blue waves logo)*.
FR*	BR Railfreight *(Grey bodyside, yellow cabs, red buffer beam/stripe at solebar level, large double-arrow logo)*.
FY	Foster Yeoman *(Blue/silver. Cast numberplates)*.
G*	BR *(Plain or two-tone green)*.
GN	Great North Eastern Railway *(Dark blue with a red stripe)*.
GS	Great Scottish & Western Railway *(Maroon)*.
GW	Great Western Trains *(Green)*.
GX	Gatwick Express *(Dark grey/white/burgundy/white)*.
GY	Eurotunnel *(Grey and yellow))*.
HB*	Hunslet-Barclay *(Two-tone grey with red solebar)*.

I*	BR InterCity *(Dark grey/white/red/light grey and yellow lower cabsides).*
IM*	BR Mainline *(Dark grey/white/red/light grey).*
IS*	BR InterCity Swallow *(Dark grey/white/red/white).*
LH*	BR Loadhaul *(Black with orange cabsides).*
MD	Mersey Travel departmental *(Yellow/black).*
MG*	BR Mainline Freight *(Two-tone grey with black cab doors and window surrounds).*
ML*	BR Mainline Freight *(Aircraft blue with silver stripe).*
MM	Midland Main Line *(Teal green with cream lower body sides and three orange stripes).*
N*	BR Network South East *(Grey/white/red/white/blue/white).*
O	Non standard liveries *(see notes in class headings for details).*
PC*	Pullman Car Company *(Umber & cream with gold lettering).*
R*	Plain red.
RF*	RFS *(Light grey with yellow and blue stripes).*
RG*	BR Parcels *(Dark grey and red).*
RP	Royal Train *(Purple, lined out in red and yellow).*
RR*	Regional Railways *(Dark Blue/Grey with light blue & white stripes, three narrow dark blue stripes at cab ends).*
RX*	Rail Express Systems *(Dark grey and red with blue markings).*
ST	Stagecoach South West Trains *(White/orange/white/red/white/blue/white).*
T*	Transrail *(Two-tone grey with Transrail logos).*
TC*	BR Civil Engineers/Transrail. *(Yellow & grey with black cab doors and window surrounds. Transrail logo).*
V	Virgin Trains *(Red & grey with three white stripes).*
W*	Waterman Railways *(Black with cream and red lining).*
WN	West Anglia Great Northern Railway *(White with blue, grey and orange stripes).*
Y	Plain yellow.

* denotes an obsolete livery style no longer used for repaints.

4. OWNER CODES

Code	Owner
50	The Fifty Fund
71	71A Locomotive Group.
90	Deltic 9000 Locomotives.
A	Angel Train Contracts.
AC	ARC.
AD	Adtranz (ABB Daimler-Benz Transportation).
AM	Alstom.
AR	Anglia Railways Train Services.
CA	Cardiff Railway Company.
CM	Cambrian Trains.
CN	The Carriage & Traction Company
CT	Central Trains.
DR	Direct Rail Services.
E	English Welsh & Scottish Railway.
ET	Eurotunnel.
EU	Eurostar (UK).
F	Forward Trust Rail.
FG	Fragonset Railways.
FL	Freightliner.
FY	Foster Yeoman.
GW	First Great Western.
GX	Gatwick Express.
HN	Harry Needle Industrial & Historical Locomotives.
HS	Harry Schneider.
IC	Imperial Chemical Industries.
LF	Alan & Tracy Lear.
ME	Merseyrail Electrics.
MM	Midland Mainline.
MO	Michael Owen.
NR	National Railway Museum.
P	Porterbrook Leasing Company.
RC	Railcare.
RF	RFS (E).
SC	Connex South Central.
SN	Société National de Chemins de fer Français.
SO	Serco Railtest.
SR	Scot Rail Railways.
SS	Sea Containers Rail Services.
SW	South West Trains.
VW	Virgin West Coast.
WN	West Anglia Great Northern Railway.

5. POOL CODES

Code   Pool

SERCO RAILTEST
CDJD   Class 08.

CAMBRIAN TRAINS
CTLO   Operational Fleet
CTLS   Stored Fleet

FREIGHTLINER
DFFT   Class 47 (with sanding equipment).
DFHZ   Class 57.
DFLC   Class 90.
DFLM   Class 47 (Multiple Working equipment).
DFLS   Class 08.
DFLT   Classes 37 & 47.
DFNC   Class 86.
DFYX   Class 47 (Stored).
DHLT   Class 47 (Awaiting maintenance).

ENGLISH WELSH & SCOTTISH RAILWAY
ENSN   Classes 08 & 09 (East Midlands).
EWEH   Classes 08 & 09 (Solent & Avon).
EWOC   Classes 08 & 09 (London, South East England & East Anglia).
FDSD   Classes 08 & 09 (South Yorkshire).
FDSI   Classes 08 & 09 (North Lincolnshire).
FDSK   Classes 08 & 09 (West Yorkshire & North Humberside)
FMSY   Classes 08 & 09 (Teesside & Tyneside).
(Continued with LBBS)

EUROSTAR (UK)
GPSN   Class 73.
GPSS   Class 08.
GPSV   Class 37.

TRAIN OPERATING COMPANIES
HASS   Scot Rail Railways Class 08.
HBSH   Great North Eastern Railway Class 08.
HEBD   Merseyrail Electrics Class 73.
HFSL   Virgin Cross Country Class 08.
HFSN   Virgin West Coast Class 08.
HGSS   Central Trains Class 08.
HISE   Midland Mainline Class 08 (Derby).
HISL   Midland Mainline Class 08 (Neville Hill).
HJSE   First Great Western Class 08 (Landore).
HJSL   First Great Western Class 08 (Laira).
HJXX   First Great Western Class 08 (Old Oak HST & St. Phillips Marsh).
HLSV   Cardiff Railway Co. Class 08 (On loan to East Somerset Railway).
HQXX   West Anglia Great Northern Railway Class 03.
HSSN   Anglia Railways Class 08.

HWSU	Connex South Central Class 09.
HYSB	South West Trains Class 73.
IANA	Anglia Railways Class 86.
JCCA	Virgin Cross Country Class 86.
JCCP	Virgin Cross Country Class 43.
JECA	Great North Eastern Railway Class 91.
JECB	Great North Eastern Railway Class 89.
JECP	Great North Eastern Railway Class 43.
JLRA	Virgin Cross Country Class 47.
JLRB	Virgin Cross Country Class 47 (Reserve fleet).
JMLP	Midland Main Line Class 43.
JVGA	Gatwick Express Class 73.
JWCA	Virgin West Coast Classes 87 & 90.
JWCP	Virgin West Coast Class 43.
JWLA	First Great Western Class 47.
JWLX	First Great Western Class 47 (Reserve fleet).
JWPA	Virgin West Coast Class 86.
JWRP	First Great Western Class 43.

ROLLING STOCK MAINTENANCE COMPANIES

KCSI	ADtranz Class 08 (Ilford).
KDSD	ADtranz Class 08 (Doncaster).
KESE	Alstom Class 08 (Eastleigh).
KGSS	Railcare Class 08 (Glasgow).
KWSW	Railcare Class 08 (Wolverton).

ENGLISH WELSH & SCOTTISH RAILWAY

(Continued from FMSY)

LBBS	Classes 08 & 09 (South & West Midlands).
LGML	Classes 08 & 09 (Scotland and Carlisle).
LNCF	Classes 08 & 09 (South Wales & West of England).
LWSP	Classes 08 & 09 (North West England).
LNWK	Class 08 (On hire to Allied Steel & Wire, Cardiff).

(Continued with WAAN)

NON TRAIN OPERATING COMPANIES

MBDL	Non TOC owned diesel locomotives (see class headings).
MBEL	Non TOC owned electric locomotives (see class headings).

LEASING COMPANIES

SAXL	Forward Trust Rail.
SBXL	Porterbrook Leasing.
SCXL	Angel Train Contracts.
SDFR	Fragonset Railways.

ENGLISH WELSH & SCOTTISH RAILWAY

(Continued from LNWK)

WAAN	Class 67.
WBAN	Class 66.
WCAN	Class 60.
WDAN	Class 59/2.
WEMF	A.C. electric locomotives (Network Freight).
WEMP	A.C. electric locomotives (Railnet & Scot Rail).
WFAN	Class 58.

WGAN	Class 56.
WHBF	Class 47 (Network Freight).
WHDA	Class 47 (VIP).
WHDC	Class 47 (On hire to Scot Rail).
WHDP	Class 47 (Railnet).
WHDT	Class 47 (Railtest).
WHMN	Class 47.
WKBN	Class 37.
WKCD	Class 37 (On hire to First North Western).
WKCN	Class 37/4.
WKFN	Class 37/5.
WKGN	Class 37/7.
WKHN	Class 37/9.
WKMB	Class 37 (RETB equipped).
WKMS	Class 37 (Sandite equipment – used in sandite season only).
WLAN	Class 33.
WMAN	Class 31.
WNWX	Main line locomotives – strategic reserve.
WNXX	Main line locomotives – stored.
WNYX	Main line locomotives – component recovery only.
WNZX	Main line locomotives – awaiting disposal.
WPAN	Class 73.
WPAR	Class 73 (Restricted use).
WSTT	Classes 08 & 09 – Remote control tests.
WSWX	Shunting locomotives – strategic reserve.
WSXX	Shunting locomotives – stored.
WSYX	Shunting locomotives – component recovery only.
WSZX	Shunting locomotives – awaiting disposal.
WTAN	Class 92 (Wembley–Frethun).
WTWN	Class 92 (WCML).

OTHER OPERATORS

XHSD	Direct Rail Services.
XHSS	Direct Rail Services – stored locos
XYPA	Mendip Rail Class 59/0.
XYPO	Mendip Rail Class 59/1.

5. DEPOT & LOCATION CODES

ode	Location	Operator
N	Allerton (Liverpool) T&RSMD	EWS
Y	Ayr SD	EWS
A	Crewe South Yard/Basford Hall Yard	Storage location only
D	Birkenhead North T&RSMD	Merseyrail Electrics
H*	Billingham TMD	ICI
M	Bournemouth T&RSMD	South West Trains
N	Bounds Green (London) T&RSMD	Great North Eastern Railway
S	Bescot (Walsall) TMD	EWS
D	Crewe Diesel TMD	EWS
E	Crewe International Electric T&RSMD	EWS
F	Cardiff Canton (Loco) TMD	EWS
P	Carlisle Upperby (closed)	Storage location only
P	Crewe CARMD	London & North Western Railway
Q	Crewe (The Railway Age) T&RSMD	Carriage & Traction
R	Doncaster TMD	EWS
Y	Derby Etches Park T&RSMD	Midland Mainline
C	Edinburgh Craigentinny T&RSMD	Great North Eastern Railway
H	Eastleigh TMD	EWS
B	Ferrybridge T&RSMD	EWS
H	Frodingham (Scunthorpe) (closed)	Storage location only
E	Gateshead (closed)	Storage location only
Y	Hornsey T&RSMD	West Anglia Great Northern Railway
G	Hither Green TMD	EWS
M	Healey Mills (Wakefield) SD	EWS
T	Heaton (Newcastle upon Tyne) T&RSMD	Northern Spirit
M	Immingham TMD	EWS
	Inverness T&RSMD	Scot Rail
D	Carlisle Kingmoor TMD	Direct Rail Services
K	Kirkdale SD	Merseyrail Electrics
R	Kidderminster	Severn Valley Railway
Y	Knottingley T&RSMD	EWS
A	Laira (Plymouth) T&RSMD	First Great Western
B	Loughborough	Brush Traction
E	Landore (Swansea) T&RSMD	First Great Western
G	Longsight Electric (Manchester) T&RSMD	Virgin Cross Country
D	Longsight Diesel (Manchester) TMD	First North Western
R	Leicester SD	EWS
A	Manchester Longsight CARMD	Virgin West Coast
D	Merehead TMD	Mendip Rail
G	Margam (Port Talbot) SD	EWS
H	Millerhill (Edinburgh) SD	EWS
L	Motherwell TMD	EWS
C	Norwich Crown Point T&RSMD	Anglia Railways
L	Neville Hill InterCity (Leeds) T&RSMD	Midland Main Line
P	North Pole International (London) T&RSMD	Eurostar (UK)
C	Old Oak Common (London) TMD	EWS

OO	Old Oak Common HST (London) T&RSMD	First Great Western
PB	Peterborough SD	EWS
PM	St. Phillips Marsh (Bristol) T&RSMD	First Great Western
RG	Reading TMD	Thames Trains
RL	Ropley	Mid Hants Railway
SD	Sellafield TMD	Direct Rail Services/RFS(E)
SE	St. Leonards T&RSMD	St. Leonards Railway Engineering
SF	Stratford (London) SD	EWS/D9000 Locomotives
SL	Stewarts Lane (London) T&RSMD	Gatwick Express
SP	Springs Branch (Wigan) CRC	EWS
SU	Selhurst (Croydon) T&RSMD	Connex South Central
TE	Thornaby T&RSMD	EWS
TM	Birmingham Railway Museum	Fragonset Railways
TO	Toton (Nottinghamshire) TMD	EWS
TS	Tyseley (Birmingham) T&RSMD	Central Trains
TT*	Toton Training School (Nottinghamshire)	Storage location only
TU*	Toton Up Yard (Nottinghamshire)	Storage location only
WA	Warrington Arpley SD	EWS
WN	Willesden (London) TMD	Virgin West Coast
ZA	Railway Technical Centre, Derby	Serco Railtest/AEA Technologies
ZB	Doncaster	RFS (E)
ZC	Crewe	Adtranz
ZF	Doncaster	Adtranz
ZG	Eastleigh	Alstom
ZH	Glasgow	Railcare
ZI	Ilford	Adtranz
ZN	Wolverton	Railcare

* denotes unofficial code.

7. DEPOT TYPE CODES

CARMD	Carriage Maintenance Depot
CRC	Component Recovery Centre
CSD	Carriage Servicing Depot
SD	Servicing Depot
TMD	Traction Maintenance depot
T&RSMD	Traction & Rolling Stock depot